Faith and the Human Enterprise

A Post-Vatican II Vision

Archbishop Rembert G. Weakland

ORBIS BOOKS

Maryknoll, New York 10545

The Catholic Foreign Mission Society of America (Maryknoll) recruits and trains people for overseas missionary service. Through Orbis Books, Maryknoll aims to foster the international dialogue that is essential to mission. The books published, however, reflect the opinions of their authors and are not meant to represent the official position of the society.

Copyright © 1992 by Most Rev. Rembert G. Weakland, O.S.B.
Published by Orbis Books, Maryknoll, NY 10545
All rights reserved
Manufactured in the United States of America

Library of Congress Cataloging-in-Publication Data

Weakland, Rembert.
    Faith and the human enterprise : a post-Vatican II vision /
Rembert G. Weakland
        p. cm.
    Includes bibliographical references.
    ISBN 0-88344-835-1 (pbk.)
    1. Catholic Church—History—1965-   2. Economic—Religious
aspects—Catholic Church.   3. Christianity and politics.   4. Church
and the world.   I. Title.
BX1390.W43   1992
261'.1—dc20   92-32884
                                                                  CIP

*To the Priests
of the Archdiocese of Milwaukee
in gratitude
for their friendship and support*

Contents

Preface

Each generation must feel that its own age is special. Although every moment of history has its challenges, some periods seem to demand decisions of such magnitude or force new ways of thinking and acting of such depth that the course of history is irrevocably changed. We Catholics who experienced Vatican Council II feel that way about our generation. We know that we have lived through, and for many years will continue to live in, times when the future direction of our Church and how it relates to the rest of society will be determined for centuries to come.

In facing the future, one of the central questions is certainly how Christian faith will influence the daily actions of millions of believers. But one must also ask how Christians will affect the values of society in general. The question for us Catholics is being posed in a different way today because of the trend in our world away from state religions to democratic constitutional governments. The Catholic Church finds itself in the midst of a new dynamic as Catholics take part in and interact with other forces that form a pluralistic, democratic society. Although this trend is well established in the United States and other parts of the globe, for the Catholic Church as a whole the positive encounter in the pluralistic, democracy is of fairly recent origin. Nevertheless, it is now a world trend that will not see a reversal. In Western Europe this trend is well-established; in Eastern Europe all indications are that it will soon be just as pervasive. Because the Catholic Church has enjoyed such a prominent place in the history of western civilization and since Catholics are taking more and more important roles in all these new and old democratic societies, it is important that the Church reflect in a special way on these new circumstances and clarify its own thinking vis-à-vis the societies enjoying these new democratic and constitutional forms of government.

The Church in the United States has an added obligation to do this kind of reflection because of its history and importance on the world scene and because Catholics form such a large segment of the population. This collection of talks and essays attempts to take up such a discussion in the light of the changes in thinking brought about by Vatican Council II. Written over a period of a decade or more, they struggle with some of the major issues any church, but especially the Catholic Church, must face in our day and in our culture. As mentioned, the starting point must be Vatican Council II and its perspectives on faith and the human enterprise, that is, on

vii

the role of the Church in the modern world. The roots of the thinking of that council are found in Catholic social teaching and its antecedent documents since the time of Pope Leo XIII (1878–1903). The questions that inevitably arise are these: What light do these democratic trends throw on the various political and economic arrangements that characterize our day, what values and disvalues do they bring to the fore, how do these values and disvalues intersect with the Christian tradition? How "catholic" or universal is the Catholic Church today? Does it have in place the structures needed to face the future and these new relationships between Church and world? Lastly, how do these democratic tendencies affect the inner life of the Church itself?

These are the questions that I have continued to struggle with in this last decade and that find their echo in these essays. I have tried to bring them up to date while leaving the substance of the thought intact.

There are many people who influenced my thinking on these subjects in the last ten years or more. Most of all, my thanks go out to the members, consultants, and staff of the drafting committee of the ad hoc Committee of the National Conference of Catholic Bishops that worked on the document *Economic Justice For All* (1986). Although I take responsibility for my own particular convictions and assessments, I learned so much from them in those endless hearings and dialogues. From among those members I would like to mention in particular: John R. Donahue, S.J., Bryan Hehir, George Higgins, David Hollenbach, S.J., Ron Krietemeyer, Martin McLaughlin, and Donald Warwick.

I would like also to express thanks to Robert Ellsberg for the idea of publishing some of my talks and essays and for his guiding hand in arranging them in some kind of logical sequence.

I become more and more convinced that there is no aspect of human life that is not touched by the vision that springs from one's faith. Reflecting on how that faith relates to society in all its ramifications brings one to the heart of the Christian mystery of the Incarnation, of God's loving plan for this world and all of us in it. Faith in God's reaching out to us humans touches every aspect of the human enterprise, which then ceases in some way to be just human but becomes a part of the divine plan. Such reflections will never end.

PART I

CHURCH AND WORLD: THE NEW MOMENT

INTRODUCTION

Any analysis of where the Catholic Church is today must begin with reference to Vatican Council II (1962–1965). That historic event is still shaping the attitude and actions of Catholics around the world today. How one interprets the documents of that council is crucial to one's perceptions of what is happening in the Church today and how the Church relates to the world.

Karl Rahner saw that council also as a symbol of a new historical moment in the life of the Church.[1] He divided the history of the Church into three phases. The first phase—very short in duration—was the moment of the Jewish roots and the first converts from Judaism. That period was immediately altered by the reception of Gentiles who were not expected to first become Jews. The battle over that principle occupied the thoughts of the participants in the first Council of Jerusalem as recorded in Acts 15 and Galatians 2. The second period corresponds to the Greco-Roman empire. In that period the Church became a part of western civilization and culture. This movement was solidified by Charlemagne and his successors. With Vatican Council II one could see a new phase beginning: The global Church, or the visibly "Catholic" Church, was evident. Now the Church is found in every culture and growing and expanding in those cultures that were not basically western. This movement demands new structures if it is to correspond to the demands of an interdependent multicultural organism.

Such an expansion into many cultures is a blessing, but it brings with it many new demands. There is always the tendency to become provincial, to regress to small, disconnected communities. It is not to be denied that most Catholics experience the Church through their individual parish, but the larger Catholic aspect of their Church is also important to their identity. In fact, at a moment when the global aspects of economy and ecology are

1

in the forefront, it is important that the "catholic" aspect of the Church also be emphasized, if the Church is to take its place as a major moral influence on the future culture that is now growing up.

One of the remarkable aspects of the post-Vatican Council II Church has been not only its global character, but also its new relationship to the world. One of the most important documents coming from that council was *Gaudium et spes* (*The Pastoral Constitution on the Church in the Modern World*). This document was not an internal reflection on the nature of the Church but how that Church should interact with the world around it. Its positive attitude, its emphasis on the dignity of the human person, its call for a humble and open stance with regard to the happenings in this world, and its reliance on the Spirit and the actions of the Spirit in the world made this document a key one for the next decades.

That document also brought to the fore the whole history of Catholic social teaching. It laid the groundwork for so many encyclicals on social justice by Pope Paul VI and Pope John Paul II that were to follow.

The three essays in this first part take up the theme of Vatican Council II, new global structures to meet the new historical moment, and the thrust for social justice and the renewal of Catholic social teaching.

CHAPTER 1

Nostalgia with a Future

Some events are turning points in history, changing people's attitudes and assumptions, altering common ways that groups have of seeing themselves and how they relate around them.[1] Vatican Council II was such an event for Catholics. It is the benchmark all must use in talking of the Catholic Church these days. No one can reflect on inner Church life or on ways the Church relates to society and world without touching on how Vatican Council II stated the question in point and indicated a solution. It may not have been a council called to promulgate dogmatic formulas; but, because it was freer and begun with a less determined scope, it reflected on a broad range of topics — almost everything that touches Catholic life — and allowed itself a more discursive and, at times, tentative way. In this it changed attitudes and perspectives. In addition, one could rightly say that Vatican Council II achieved a broader scope than that of dealing with internal concerns of the Church itself, because it brought to the consciousness of Catholics the need to reflect on how Catholicism relates to the other Christian bodies, to the major great religions, and to the world in which the drama of salvation takes place. Because it took a new and fresh look at all those relationships, it challenged, one could also say it changed, the agenda for all peoples of all faiths as it sought a new relationship with all its partners. In this sense it produced consequences that have affected everyone.[2]

Moreover, each part of the Church found itself at a different historical juncture when Vatican Council II opened, creating circumstances that altered its reception and interpretation throughout the Catholic world. The Catholic Church in the U.S.A., for example, was not ready for these changes. It had had a prosperous history in the last century, increasing rapidly as Catholic immigrants poured into the borders of this nation. It had built schools, founded hospitals, and helped its members move ahead in a society that seemed to offer limitless possibilities. Returning from World War II, Catholics took advantage of the many opportunities for higher education, lost their immigrant roots, and advanced rapidly into all

3

strata of American society. Their children, they hoped, would enjoy, from a material point of view, a better life than they or their grandparents had experienced, most of whom had suffered and sacrificed much through the depression years, swelling the ranks of the labor unions and edging ahead in local politics. They passed in those post-World War II decades from being an immigrant Church to being an established and accepted one.

The postwar period was, for the most part, an optimistic era for the Church in the U.S.A. and for its people, one of feverish building, too, as its members became more numerous and more affluent. There was little questioning of the basic spirituality, structures, or doctrines handed on to the faithful by their clergy. Their concern was mostly in consolidating, from a material point of view, their position in the local communities. The pastor still dominated the scene; lay people were his assistants. The priests got their orders from the bishops who, in turn, got theirs from the Pope. Sunday Mass, meatless Fridays, and the like were the marks of Catholic identity. In some respects, Catholics felt that this monolithic nature of their Church would remain unchanged forever. Having such a short historical memory, U.S. Catholics felt that their Church had always been as they then knew it to be and that it would, thus, remain immutable.

But underneath, many thinkers knew that the Church had not yet made its peace with the modern age that placed much emphasis on science, on rugged individualism and personal freedom, on democratic processes. As Catholics received higher educational degrees from the best universities in the country and as their own intellectual climate rose, they began to question many aspects of the rigidity of discipline and thought that they had known as children. Under the surface, then, all was not quiet; Catholics could not remain unaffected by attitudes and assumptions of the world around them. Vatican Council II became the vehicle for uncovering that unrest and naming it. It was to be the council for modern times.

COUNCIL FEVER

Vatican Council II (1962–1965) played itself out on the world stage while we here in the U.S.A. were still living in the afterglow of the Kennedy period and were still traumatized by the vivid memory of his death and burial. We were just coming out of the shock of those events, having lost our political innocence, but it was an optimistic period, since we had not yet experienced the turbulence of the late sixties and the early seventies. We, too, were enamored with the personality of the wise and affable Pope John XXIII, one who was beloved by the whole world and all faiths. As a historian, he understood the need for the Church to come to terms with the world around it and trusted in the guidance of the Spirit as he opened Vatican Council II on October 11, 1962. His untimely death in the middle of the council permitted us to come to know Pope Paul VI, elected in the spring of 1963, who vowed to continue the council begun by his predecessor.

He was a different sort of person, much more given to introspection and less jovial by nature, but of keen intellect, with a sense and flare for the modern, especially in art. Many felt he vacillated at times, siding now with one group, now with another, but keeping the Church united and undivided became the main goal and thrust of his pontificate as he completed the council and then set about to implement its decrees.

December 1963 marked the promulgation of the first documents of Vatican Council II, one on the reform of the liturgy and one on social communications.[3] These documents seemed far apart in tone and content, but they were to be but the beginning of a whole series of documents that were then being outlined—one on the Church, one on divine revelation, one on religious liberty, and so on. Here in the U.S.A. a certain excitement filled the air. It was all so new to us. We eagerly and zealously read Xavier-Rynne to find out what the inner workings of the council might be like and reveled in every aspect of the controversies that surrounded the proceedings.[4] Some of our Protestant friends chided us that we were being too optimistic and almost idealistic about the Church and the future. They reminded us of sin and suffering; but we felt that that was too "Lutheran" an interpretation of both Church and world. We set about to update our Church in every way requested.

In the U.S.A., probably because our roots were not that deep, we had fewer problems in throwing off centuries of baggage. In spite of the rigidity of the Church as we had known it, or perhaps because of that rigidity, we took up the renewal of the Church in earnest. We wanted to see our Church as relevant to the modern world and as taking its role in the future development of civilization. So many of the aspects of Vatican Council II seemed to us to be in consonance with our American tradition, especially those areas that emphasized the role of the laity in both Church and world. Having just come out of our immigrant, more closed-off status, we were ripe for a vision of Church that permitted more involvement with the world. The election of John Kennedy had changed how we saw United States society and our role in it. Since World War II we had been steadily assuming more and more important roles in society, business, and scholarly professions. Vatican Council II, in that respect, came at just the right moment of our history and of our relationship to United States society. We were not sure where it would all lead us, but we were not afraid of the challenge. I am also sure that the fervor with which the Church in the U.S.A. embraced Vatican Council II centered around the way in which Catholics could simultaneously embrace and integrate into their Church life so many of the aspects of their American heritage, especially the democratic processes and the sense of equality.

Those council years were exciting ones. As a young man of 36, elected in 1963 as abbot of a vital and strong Benedictine monastery, St. Vincent in Latrobe, Pennsylvania, I relished all that was happening. The documents came out so fast, and some were of such density, and one could also say novelty, that it would have been impossible for the members of any church to understand them and then absorb them. Few of the documents were really read and studied at that time. Stories abounded about them, how they were written by committees of experts or *periti*, discussed on the floor with certain animation (we all came to know the characters involved on the different sides of each issue), and then solemnly promulgated by the Pope. In so many respects it was a shame that these documents were not published more systematically, put into more digestible form for the average Catholic, and thus absorbed more gradually. But that was not possible, and so we all hoped that with time we would be able to study them as we should. In the meantime, we relied on journalistic accounts of what had happened and how bishops had reacted. It should also be said, in all honesty, that often the true contents of the documents did not become known to the person in the pew, but the journalistic version, bereft of any subtlety or nuance. General impressions replaced accuracy in the minds of many. We still suffer from this lack of a thorough analysis, so that in the minds of many there remain just those general, and not always too accurate, impressions.

Unfortunately, in the U.S.A. in the 1960s we were not, for the most part, intellectually prepared for the new vision that the documents expounded. Because of the modernist purge at the beginning of this century, our seminaries had been sealed off from the ferment that had been taking place in Europe in the twenties and thirties. The war had interrupted these theological advances, but they were resurrected again in the late forties and fifties. The U.S. seminaries and schools of higher learning did not become a part of these new currents. Some, nevertheless, had reached us through enlightened centers, teachers, and pastors, especially in the area of liturgy and biblical studies. Although such powerful centers of learning as St. John's Abbey in Collegeville, Minnesota, brought the very best of this new thinking in liturgy into the U.S., those new ideas had not reached the entire Church but had remained an oasis among certain groups of religious, pastors, and other connoisseurs. This new thinking had not yet reached the masses and was seen as peripheral to the life of the Church, if not characterized as elitist.

Nevertheless, the council brought with it a new fervor and a new élan that the Church in the U.S.A. had not seen for many a year. Although our seminaries had simply not prepared our priests for the vast new ideas and given them the theological context, they quickly and readily embraced them. Men and women religious, in particular the latter, were in the forefront of those who took the council seriously and began, through many workshops and seminars, to study the documents and implement their spirit. In so many ways, those were heady days. I recall the fervor with which we were writing new music for the liturgy in the monastery at Latrobe. It seemed that a whole new repertoire was needed overnight. Some of our work was surprisingly good; most exhibited trained craftsmanship but demonstrated little inspiration. We dreamt of an Elizabethan age for English in the liturgy, one that would involve the finest of poets and the best of composers. We were waiting for the nod to get started in earnest.

THE AIMS OF VATICAN COUNCIL II

The aims of Vatican Council II were spelled out in the opening paragraph of the very first document of the council, namely that on liturgy, *Sacrosanctum Concilium*. In its own words, the council thus stated its goals: "It is the intention of this holy council to improve the standard of daily Christian living among Catholics; to adapt those structures which are subject to change so as better to meet the needs of our time; to encourage whatever can contribute to the union of all who believe in Christ; and to strengthen whatever serves to call all people into the embrace of the Church."[5] These were vast and inspiring aims; they involved a pastoral thrust (to impart an ever-increasing vigor to the Christian life); they implied updating the institutions of the Church, bringing them into the twentieth century; they demanded ecumenism and a quest for unity; they saw a new evangelization. These were fresh and all-embracing aims.

To support these goals a series of documents were produced by experts — the *periti* — and then amended, and finally voted on by the bishops. Some of these documents were called constitutions and were of a more theological nature; others were called decrees or declarations. Their content was both pastoral and theological. One only has to look at the *Constitution on the Church (Lumen gentium)* or at *The Dogmatic Constitution on Divine Revelation (Dei verbum)* to see their doctrinal depth. The bishops were aware of the fact that good pastoral practice rests on good theology. I would like to sum up the main themes that weave through the documents of Vatican Council II in four categories.[6]

The first theme would be a new way of looking at the Church itself. Ecclesiology is at the basis of the changes of all thinking after Vatican Council II. By beginning the document on the Church, *Lumen gentium*, with the concept of the People of God and not with the Pope and the hierarchy, the bishops made a very clear and challenging statement about the nature of the Church itself. The concept of communion (often cited in its Latin form as *communio* to avoid confusion with the Eucharist and to avoid sociological overtones that words such as *fellowship* connote) becomes in the post-Vatican II Church the preferred noun to describe the nature of the Church. Although the council used the term *People of God* to describe that *communio* among all God's people, unfortunately since then there has been a tendency in official documents to try to avoid it. But the people still find it the most attractive phrase to describe the Church, and it has not and will not disappear from use. Although the role of the hierarchy is not slighted, all God's people become responsible for the Church, just as they are called equally to holiness. From this more communal definition of Church derives the emphasis on collegiality among the bishops and such concepts as co-responsibility for the mission of the Church shared by all the faithful. Suddenly the role of the laity, because of their baptism, becomes uppermost in the description of the functioning Church.

One could say that a new emphasis on the importance of the local church is also found in that first chapter of the document on the Church. It is not a denial of the importance of the Universal Church; but that document begins with people, all the faithful, and points out the need to see the assembled community, especially at the Eucharist, as the living cell of the Holy Spirit, before going on to delineate specific roles in the Church.

These changes in perspective have not been easily assimilated by all of us. We fear the new and often cling to the old, or at least romanticize the past and want to look back to it. I smile often when I receive a lecture from someone pushing the concept of co-responsibility and then, when something goes wrong, find that the same person will easily and immediately blame the bishop! Or, at times, these same advocates of co-responsibility, when they want something accomplished in the Church, will seek to have it mandated by the bishop! We so easily forget the new model and still like to use the episcopal power for our own ends. Slowly, however, since Vatican Council II the people are learning to assume responsibility for their decisions.

These changes of perspective have been important here in the U.S.A. because they play on our social traditions and sensitivities toward democratic principles. They were, thus, welcomed by Americans in general. They have affected how Americans think the Church should now operate today on all levels. At times, some have not made proper distinctions between democracy as it has been traditionally lived in the U.S.A. and the traditions of the Church. Still the attempt to recapture some of the nature of the Church and the role of all as described in the Acts of the Apostles has been a gain, even if it has led at times to some exaggerations.

Vatican Council II also outlines a new relationship between the Church and the world. The prime document for this perspective is certainly *The Pastoral Constitution on the Church in the Modern World (Gaudium et spes)*. In so many ways this document is not a finished product; it seems more like a first essay, a tentative attempt to look at the role of the Church in society in a new light. It is a modest document, but a very inspiring one. The Church now does not attempt to have all the answers but rather to be a companion on the journey with all those who create the history of this world. The evils of the world are not hidden, but there reigns a positive attitude toward the engagement of the Church in the projects of this world. That the Church has a social mission is apparent from this document, but that mission does not correspond to a purely natural end. The document does not always seem to be clear on the relationship between the aims of this world and the Kingdom of God, but that the two are intimately connected is evident. This model is not one of establishing a place for God's Kingdom in a world apart, as it were, but one which sees the interpenetration between the history of this world and the working out of God's Kingdom.

This document also gives a unique basic perspective to the whole relationship between Church and world: It sees the human person as the center of the world. It sees the value and worth and dignity of the human person as the ultimate value to be worked toward in this world and in the social relationships within this world. Such a view has had a positive impact on the way the Church has dealt with such issues as abortion, euthanasia, and the like. On the other hand, such a strong anthropocentrism has been seen as a deterrent in the continued search for a theology that corresponds to ecological concerns.

One should make bold to say that the third unique contribution of Vatican Council II lies in the concept of religious freedom. The document that treated this subject, *Declaration on Religious Freedom* (*Dignitatis humanae*), has been a bit neglected by us Americans because we take religious freedom so much for granted. We see this document as the special contribution of the Church of the U.S.A. to the work of Vatican Council II, and indeed it was. Many non-Americans saw clearly the special importance and significance of both the concept and the document. It points out the need for religious freedom if the human person is to be and to become the kind of free agent which God created people to be. It also sees that religious beliefs cannot be forced on anyone; they demand a free and informed consent of the individual conscience. There is no wonder that Archbishop Marcel Lefebvre, later to become the leader of the Tridentine movement that has rejected most of the perspectives of Vatican Council II, opposed this document when it was first discussed and consistently did so all his life. He adhered to the concept that wrong has no rights and must be stamped out. To him, religious freedom was license to do wrong and, therefore, a concept that is not Christian.

Built into this document is the acceptance of a de facto pluralism in the expression of religious belief in any society. Conscience cannot be forced. It seems evident that this document cannot be reconciled with any theory that would postulate a kind of Catholic State in the future. It does not, however, spell out in practice how such pluralism would function or the role of the Catholic Church in such a society. It is clear that it does not rule out the possibility of the Church as one of the participants in the "public square," but it does exclude the suppression of other views. The implications of this important document have not been totally worked out.

Lastly, Vatican Council II took a new and positive view of other religions. Ecumenism is at the heart of the documents and the approaches of Vatican Council II. Not only did it open the doors to a new way of looking at the truths of faith and of the relationship between the Catholic Church and the other Christian churches, but it also began a fresh way of seeing the other great religions on this globe. Since then, ecumenism has been no longer an academic study relegated to theological schools, but a movement toward unity that is demanded by Christ himself. Ecumenism is an attitude that demands that at all times we seek to be one with other Christians. It also means that we do not neglect the good qualities of other religions but treat them in a way that recognizes such positive elements, names them as authentic ecclesial elements, and embraces them as such. Working for and praying for Christian unity has become the clearest sign of the postconciliar Church.

One would have to admit, however, that the ecumenical thrust has affected the Church in the U.S.A. in ways not at first foreseen. In countries such as Poland and Italy, where Catholicism is the only major religious force, Catholic identity has not been affected by this ecumenical thrust. In a country such as the U.S.A., however, where the immigrant Catholic Church strove for over a century to identify itself over against the Protestant "WASP" majority, ecumenism has put some Catholics into a form of identity crisis. Catholics must now accept that they have much in common with Protestants, especially after their re-discovery of the Bible in this post-Vatican II age and through their mutual involvement in so many social and charitable projects. They must cease to identify themselves over against Protestantism and begin to accept those traditions and values which all Christians hold in common. Some have not been able to accept this new form of identification without inner turmoil and a certain sense of uneasiness.

THE INTERVENING YEARS

What has happened between the end of the council and today? Some would give the impression that the Holy Spirit abandoned the Church after the council, repudiating all that happened after its closing. Such a view is certainly not very Catholic or traditional. Historians tell us that after every council there has been a period of turmoil as the Church tried to assimilate the new doctrines and reduce them to appropriate pastoral practices. After each council there have always been those who refused to accept the new doctrines or the new perspectives on old teachings, and who easily separated themselves from the renewed or reformed Church. One also saw this happen after Vatican Council II.

One would have to admit also that some went too far in their interpretations, acting as if the whole of the Catholic tradition was up for grabs. To say, however, that the conservative positions taken after Vatican Council II were but a reaction to the excesses does not, it seems to me, correspond to the facts of history. The conservative groups, such as those who followed Msgr. Lefebvre, existed before, during, and after the council. In so many ways we are too close to write the history of those intervening years and too emotionally tied into the renewal of the Church to be objective and to have the vision needed; but they were most important years, and the experiments—yes, even the excesses—contributed much to our understanding of the council and its importance.

After the council certain events and changes happened both in Church and world that influenced the implementation of Vatican Council II. In the United States, the council came at a most propitious moment. A new generation of Catholics, more educated and more affluent, had risen up. After World War II, many Catholics, spurred on by the admonitions of the good sisters who taught them in grade school and high school, took advantage of opportunities for higher education and began to take more influential places in the fabric of U.S. society. Gradually Catholics were found in all aspects of the political scene, in business, in the arts, in education. One could say that Catholics had come out of the ghetto and were taking places of responsibility in the U.S. society.

In 1963, good Pope John XXIII, in his encyclical *Pacem in terris*, had noted some special signs of our times. These signs were to become evident and play an important role in those postconciliar years. They serve as a good guide for discussing trends in the post-Vatican II period. They are not, strictly speaking, trends in the Church; but because they are determinant thrusts in society, they affect the life of the Church, as well. I will use them here as a basis for analysis.

First, Pope John XXIII talked about the new role of the working class. He noted that it was changing rapidly and assuming more and more power in the culture. Such a change was visible among the Catholics of the U.S.A., as well. The good pontiff noted their desire to control the decisions that affected their lives. This trend has had its repercussions also on the Church in the U.S.A. in the post-Vatican II period. As strange as it may seem to some, the changes in liturgy—always the barometer of Church life—had to meet the demands of this middle class and their tastes. The introduction of so many popular elements, from guitars to ballad-style songs, is the proof of this trend. The innate democratic tendencies of this class also made them ready for the parish council movements and the movements of shared responsibility in Church governance in general.

The changes that have taken place within that class, however, have not ended. We see many of them in the next generation becoming very prominent persons in our society, and others becoming more and more dejected. The economic changes that altered the scene in the U.S.A. in the last decade have affected that class drastically. But that split has affected liturgy, too, since there is a rising aversion to these more popular elements introduced a decade earlier. Moreover, there is also a trend to more secular corporate management principles in Church structures. Some of these changes have come about because of the restraints put on Church structures in 1983, with the introduction of a new Code of Canon Law, that have restricted the expressions of co-responsibility between clergy and lay for the mission of the Church. These evolutions are still in progress. I expect that continued tensions will abound, since the Church is so deeply affected by changes within the society itself.

Next Pope John XXIII talked of the new role of women in society. How often that has been mentioned since then! In the Synod of Bishops held in Rome in 1971, it was one of the themes most discussed. A commission to study the role of women in society and Church was called for by the participating bishops, but none was named. The role of women still remains the major challenge for the Church in our day. The negativity expressed against the Church today centers so often around this issue of the restricted role of women in Church governance and Church ministry. The Church has not been able to be a positive voice in society in this regard because it is seen as a negative witness, not practicing what it preaches. How women view themselves is also a divisive question among women in the Church. Some sensitivities have evolved in the use of language that seemed demeaning to women, but such progress is small and insignificant compared to the larger issues at stake. This theme has dominated the inner discussions within the Church in this post-Vatican period, and the next decades will see more of the same, unless—what is not an impossibility—many of the women seeking their rightful place in a clerically dominated society decide to just leave and drift away. The next decades will be dominated by this theme, which will continue to divide us as Church and weaken our ability to be proclaimers of the Good News for our days.

Thirdly, Pope John XXIII mentioned the trend toward independence of nations. This movement did not affect us much in the U.S.A., but it certainly was dramatic in third-world areas. Liberation theology is an important product of reflection on this phenomenon. Later in the same encyclical, Pope John mentioned another sign of the times similar to this one: the interdependency among nations. These factors were to dominate the scene from a cultural and economic point of view for the next two decades. We live, in fact, in that atmosphere today. After the colonial period and political independence, third-world nations often found themselves in an economic dependency that has curtailed their freedom and development. Their large debts following the oil cartels of the early 1970s is an even tighter strait-jacket.

In our own nation we found ourselves moving toward more and more disillusionment after the Vietnam War. We also saw a strong conservative movement taking over through its reaction to the liberalism of the postwar period. We are still in the middle of that trend.

The Church in the U.S.A. has undergone similar transformations because of its new role in politics. Differing political positions among the faithful were the source of divisions within the ecclesial body. The question of the relationship between Church and world became a very practical question, and the answers were played out in the political arena in very concrete issues—abortion, capital punishment, nuclear war, economic aims, welfare, and the like. One of the hottest debates in the Church has been its role in those questions that affect the moral and ethical values that influence society and how those values are to be embodied in public policy. These still remain as some of the thorniest issues to be constantly faced.

There are many other trends in society and world that have affected the renewal of the Church in the decades after Vatican Council II. In the world, one would immediately mention the breakup of the Eastern Socialist bloc. In the Church, several factors have played dominant roles: the types of clergy named as bishops, the increasing concern about financial restraints at all levels of Church life, the shortage of vocations to religious life and priesthood, and the concern for Catholic identity and orthodoxy in Catholic universities and institutions. To be accurate in such a description, one would have to outline also the "restoration" endeavors spoken of by Cardinal Ratzinger of the Congregation for the Doctrine of the Faith, which have become the thread used by historians, especially European, to characterize the pontificate of Pope John Paul II.[7] This attempt seems to be inspired by the desire to turn back the clock, not to the pre-Vatican II period, but to the texts themselves, as if there had been no development since then, to interpret them in the light of only one side of the debate during the council itself, and to begin the implementation all over again, but in a controlled and highly centralized way. It is not clear if this is the mind of the present Pope or not, since he has not clearly articulated such a course. An ambivalence seems to remain, as the Pope's words calling for reform do not always coincide with his appointments and actions. His calling of a special Synod of Bishops on the twentieth anniversary of the council pointed to a more open direction, and many hoped this would result in a less restrictive implementation of the council's aims.

RECAPTURING THE SPIRIT

Nevertheless, when Pope John Paul II called the Extraordinary Synod of 1985, twenty years after the council, to capture some of its spirit, one could see at once the difference in attitudes and atmosphere that had risen in the Church and the world during the intervening twenty years. Gone were the élan and the optimism. Gone also was the level of trust. Sides had been taken about the postconciliar development and were frozen into place, and the battle lines seemed real and hotly contested. Yet the Holy Father knew that the council, as he said, remains the "fundamental event in the life of the contemporary church." He also wrote about his purpose in calling the synod: "We must ceaselessly refresh ourselves at that source, and all the more so when meaningful dates, such as those of this year, grow near and stir memories and emotions from that truly historical event."[8]

By calling the synod, he stated that he hoped to revive the atmosphere of communion that had been seen in the council; he wanted to renew the exchange of information and experiences about its application over these two decades; he wanted to deepen the engrafting of Vatican Council II into the Church's life in the light of the new situation in which the Church finds itself two decades later. That synod tried to blend the different trends that had arisen in the interpretation of the council since it was held.[9] Thus, the synod recognized the concept of the mystery of the Church and the call to all of holiness. It still did not neglect the concept of communion (*communio*) that had been accentuated since the council. It acknowledged the renewal in the Word of God as proclaimed in the liturgy and the renewed importance of Sacred Scripture in the lives of the faithful. It also emphasized the role of the Church in its mission to the world. These basic threads of Vatican II were not to be lost, even though there remains much to be done to reconcile all of them. Unfortunately, that special synod had little effect on the life of the Church. It did not reach the grass roots and the thinking of the people in general, already perhaps a bit inured to the many papal and Roman documents and pronouncements and a bit alienated from the center.

One can rightly ask, then, if the tensions perceived by the synod were really solved. The vital question of the role of the Church to the world and its problems remains to be worked out. The whole debate over liberation theology has not subsided; it has just gone underground. In our own country, there still are many who would deny any role to the Church in shaping societal issues other than purely theoretical and doctrinal considerations. Defining the delicate balance between these elements as they touch political debate is yet ahead of us. We would all admit that the scope of the Church is not to be limited to this world, that the Church has a very special role peculiar to it that involves the final fulfillment of God's Kingdom, and that it must work toward that end. Yet we also know that the creating of a world of justice and love here and now is the preparation for that final end. The eschatological aim of the Church is not separated from the here-and-now existence of the members of the Church.

Seeking communion within the Church is not easy when people have different expectation levels of the Church and when individual needs seem to dominate. That unity must be sought without destroying the differences that are legitimate and lawful. Such a balance is not easy, and we are far from finding it.

Perhaps, however, the greatest danger and evil today lies hidden under the lack of a positive morale or desire to continue the renewal of the Church and its structures that were postulated in the first paragraph of the first document of Vatican Council II. There is a certain discouragement in the Church, especially among priests. Many feel that they gave their lives to relearning their theology so they could pastorally implement the desires of the council. Now they wonder if it may have been in vain, that the council is being lost, or that we are returning to preconciliar days in thoughts and attitudes. This is a serious danger, and perhaps the only important one.

In any case, the special Synod of 1985 failed to unify the Church and give a single interpretation to Vatican Council II. Its effects among the faithful have been imperceptible. It did not accept historical realities—where the People of God were—but thought it could reverse the strong trends that were dormant in the Church since the turn of this century but were stirred up by Vatican Council II.

But the strength of the Vatican II documents and spirit of that council do live on. These documents are quoted often and remain the source of the vision that most people in the Church have today. They are used time and again by pastors and theologians; they are now the subject of endless examination by all. In that sense they have not lost their vigor and influence.

LOOKING TOWARD THE FUTURE

I would suggest that the following points or resolutions must be ours now in the 1990s, if we will be true to our past and if we wish to build a future that is consistent yet open to the Kingdom of the risen Lord.

First of all, we must maintain a positive attitude toward Vatican Council II and what it intended to do for the Church. We must not permit ourselves to be discouraged or weak in trust and faith. The council documents must be the basis of our theology now and in the future. They may sound stilted and be difficult to read, but their truths are the only way we will bring the Church into dialogue with our century. I do not know how I could have survived the last two decades without the documents of Vatican Council II. They are truly a gift from God. We must not let ourselves be deceived by those who would repudiate the council or say that, since it was not dogmatic but pastoral, it did not bring any new insights into the living of our faith. This is simply not true. The council was indeed very dogmatic, and one can never separate good theology from good practice.

Secondly, one must not repudiate the implementation of the council during the decades that followed it. Many aspects of the council simply were incomplete. Time after time the documents called for a commission of implementation. Pope Paul VI set up many commissions to make that implementation come true. The documents from those commissions are indeed very valid and very useful. They are the source of any authentic interpretation of Vatican Council II. The Holy Spirit did not leave the Church after the voting on the last document of the council. The guided implementation of the documents and their pastoral working-out are valid moments in the history of our Church and not to be made light of. The abuses are to be acknowledged, but these do not obscure the valid implementation that has taken place. We are also to be grateful to those theologians who have given their lives to that implementation. We can also learn much from the years of experience that we have had as Church in fulfilling the wishes of the council. Any "restoration" movement that does not take into account history will fail. One can never go back into history and relive it; we must accept living where we are.

Thirdly, we must never forget that the scope or purpose of the conciliar documents is that of increasing our holiness. Their living out should lead to greater personal holiness and to a more loving community of faith. This deeper spirituality cannot be ignored in favor of some external plan or program. Are we a holier people? Are we a more charitable people? Are we a more just people? These are the kinds of questions we must still be asking ourselves. Have the changes remained merely external, or have we truly interiorized them so that they are our very way of thinking and acting?

Lastly, we must still be positive about the role of the Church in relationship to the world. The documents of Vatican Council II called the Church "the Sacrament of the World." We must appreciate this very special role for the Church and not be ashamed to proclaim it and seek to implement it. That role cannot be purely a political one, nor is it a purely spiritual one. The Church is always seen in relationship to the Kingdom of God, a kingdom that began with the coming of Christ and will reach its final and full realization only with His second coming. But the here and now is where that Kingdom is realized and worked out. Thus the world here and now is indeed important for God, for Christ and his mission, and thus for the Church. Working for justice, trying to realize the Isaian vision of a world of peace and righteousness, is our task. We must not be deterred from speaking out about injustice because we might offend a political platform or challenge those in power.

On a more positive note, we must be a part of all those movements that seek to bring justice to the poor and the marginalized. We must encourage those seeking their human dignity in a world where they do not count. When we teach God's love to the poor, we are also helping them realize that they are indeed worth something: They are God's chosen ones. In so many ways this is revolutionary, but it is as God intended it to be. When we encourage others to take their rightful place in society, we help them to be instruments in God's Kingdom.

I am one of those who feels that, since Vatican Council II, we have emphasized too much the role of the laity within the Church and have not helped the faithful see that their role, too, *within* the Church, like that of the clergy, should be a means of helping all the faithful and themselves, as well, to take their role *in society*. We have been too inward in our vision and not open to the transformation of the world, which is the task of the lay Christian. Bringing to that world today the values and vision of the gospel is the charge we all have. I am convinced that the dominant culture in the world today is our own American culture. It is, thus, our duty to make that culture the expression of gospel values. In this way we do indeed evangelize.

In the 1960s the world was full of positive and idealistic thinkers, within the Church and in the general society. Today it seems that prophets of doom have a wider audience; there is less optimism. Perhaps I could say that there is less vision, too. But the future is in the hands of those with realistic dreams, those who have been able to sustain their vision in spite of so many signs that are depressing. The future is never created by those who only tear down, by those who only criticize, by those who only find fault with what others are attempting to do. This is, moreover, not a moment for self-pity; it is a time for reflection, for acting, for creating. The atmosphere is more sober, the challenge to sustain a vision more demanding, but the need is, thus, all the more clear.

We have to absorb the documents and spirit of Vatican Council II and make them our own. That council planted a seed; we have yet to reap its fruit. It is our role to continue to cultivate the growing plant.

CHAPTER 2

Catholicism Today

A New Agenda

Wherever I go these days I sense that people are asking the same provocative question: What is the role of the Church today with regard to the central problems that this globe must face for the future?[1] Some formulate the question this way: What does it mean for the Church today to say that it has a message, a gospel message, for the world? It seems to me that this question stems from an inner need for clearer vision at this moment of history, one that reflects more on the new signs of the times with regard to where the world is heading and a corresponding new agenda for the Church. These are important questions for our laity as they assume more and more influential positions in national and world leadership.

People sense that there is a specific and important role that the Church could play, especially after its assertions in *The Pastoral Constitution on the Church in the Modern World* that the Church's history is intertwined with that of the world itself, so that the world's griefs and sorrows as well as the world's joys and triumphs become part of the Church's own history. Members of the Church are searching for the answer to this question, an answer that will unite them in a common cause, that will be beneficial for the world, and that will also be a clear articulation of the mission of the Church as a part of the world.

There are some, it is true, who have given up on the whole catholic nature of the Church and believe the future lies on the local level, that the tendency in history should be toward decentralization, not deeper unification. Although there is much truth in this theory and there should be a stronger regard for the local level and its autonomy, the very nature of the Church demands a response to its more global or catholic nature. One vision does not deny the other. A strong worldwide influence of the Church will be dependent on its inner local strength and the vitality of its parts.

18

HESITANT ANSWERS

Most answers that one hears from Church leaders are attempts to be positive but cautious about the role that the Church could play with regard to the world here and now. Many feel that there is a mission for the Church, that it is the task of the Church to be a "Sacrament to the world," as Vatican Council II put it, a sign or witness of what the world could be like if it were to accept its transcendent destiny. But most answers then go on to place many qualifying "buts" after those positive assertions, clichéd, cautionary phrases about how the purpose of the Church is essentially eschatological (as if oriented only to a remote, distant, and disconnected future), or spiritual, or apolitical. Thus they imply that the Church can give no positive answers that would be relevant or concrete for this moment of history. Many of the criticisms against liberation theology give this negative impression. The argument sounds like this: Yes, indeed, salvation has something to do with this world. Yes, Jesus did have a preferential option for the poor. Yes, the Church does seek a just society. But that is all for the end of time. Till then. . . .

A very different kind of answer is given by some today. They want to be positive but so easily put the Church against the world, as if the Church were not to be tainted by the world. Rather, they imply that the duty of the Church is to seek to create on its own an alternative to the structures of this present world. Most of the answers from Fundamentalists and from those Catholics associated theologically with them often take this "over against" position. In such a perspective, striving for orthodoxy and maintaining a high degree of noncontamination is the program that should unite us. They feel everything in the world is immoral and in the hands of the powers of evil, so one has to reject this world and create a whole new "Christian" society. Unfortunately, this group seems to have the answers already made; they allow no time for hesitancy or experimentation. They also sense no need or obligation to pursue the question of inculturation.

The two positions just described seem to be the cause of either fear or indifference among many Catholics. The strongest fear in one camp is that the Church will lose its futurist, eschatological thrust if it gets too involved with the present course of this world. In the other camp the fear is that the Church will lose its already realized eschatological integrity and its purity of doctrine if it pursues any association at all with this contemporary evil world. Many of the laity become indifferent when they see that the problems over which the institutional Church is squabbling have no relation to their lives and their concerns. For these people both eschatological orientations render the Church so totally disconnected from the here and now as to be irrelevant.

Moreover, these answers are not helpful for all those lay Catholics who must live in and associate with the world in a very real and vital way. They sense that both of these approaches lead nowhere. They are not positive visions for the future, but fear-driven reactions. Moreover, they have built-in tendencies to divisiveness. In such a context one can never be really orthodox enough; one can never be cautious enough. There always arises the division between the pure and the more pure. Such tendencies lead to ever-tightening restraints that cause new divisions.

POSITIVE APPROACHES

As Church, we need today a new and positive approach, one that will unite us; we need a new and hopeful vision of our role toward this world here and now. Otherwise, I fear that each Christian will go his or her own way. There are many Catholics in prominent and important positions in our society today. They want their lives to be significant for the world and cannot be told that their efforts are insignificant or irrelevant as we wait for the eschaton. Nor can they be told that all the answers are already available, that there is no more need to think, to search out how the gospel relates to our world today. They are too bright to reject all the incredible discoveries of our age as being of no import to God and God's Kingdom. They do not deny that God's Kingdom has indeed a transcendent and eschatological aim, but ask what the fact of the Incarnation—God becoming flesh—means here and now, under these precise nonrecurring circumstances of history.

I sense that some are seeking this unifying program under words such as *evangelization*. This is a positive term, and it is also vague enough to include everything. In that respect, it is indeed a good rallying point. For the members of the Church it can mean an internal, continual conversion; it can mean a positive thrust to bring the gospel to our daily lives; it can mean bringing the gospel to our culture and the world. However, the problem with the word is that it is used so much by the Evangelicals and Fundamentalists that even Catholics using it can easily imply acceptance of those approaches that see the Church as over against the world. The evangelization rhetoric is often that of identifying the "saved" as against everyone else; it is an approach that can be aggressive, harsh, and unecumenical. Often it makes no effort to evangelize the culture. In fact, the culture it uncritically and often unsuspectingly transports with it is often vacuous and anything but ennobling or enduring. Often it is difficult to see in it the genuine multi-century Catholic tradition.

For the above reasons, we need a new agenda, one that is positive but discriminating, true to the gospel and tradition but not afraid to raise the right questions for Church and culture today, one that is humble but not fearful. It must be an agenda that is neither crippled by cautiousness nor radically indifferent about the course of human history and cultural change. In this sense the present *kairos* can become truly the Catholic moment.

A NEW UNIVERSALISM

Our first task is to analyze the historical situation we find ourselves in, with regard to both Church and world. The mission of the Church is bound up with history; we are a historical Church. The death and resurrection of the Lord are real, pivotal events that inaugurated the Church in history, affected the course of this world, and continue to touch our lives in the here and now.

One of the distinguishing marks of our times as Church is that we are finally becoming truly a catholic Church. Karl Rahner, in his observations about the uniqueness of Vatican Council II, pointed this out clearly.[2] For the first time we now must take up the agenda of what it means to be a catholic or universal community of faith—a world-Church. Our unity will no longer be sustained by the cultural expressions of western civilization. The bonds of the western empire now make no sense to Catholicism. The gospel has been implanted in nations and among races who do not share most of our past history. In their regard, the gospel must strike a different chord, coming as it does at a different moment in their own histories. It is a new moment for them, as well. Must they accept all the baggage of our history to receive that gospel message? Instinctively we say, of course not. But what does such a reply really mean? Are we willing to make distinctions so that the younger churches can have the freedom of inculturation that will make them credible in their new historical context of postcolonialism and new nationalism?

For the U.S.A. the problem is not just one of internationalization, but also one that affects the internal life of the Church here. The question of cultural pluralism is constantly raised by the Black, Hispanic, and Native American communities, as they seek to find their home in a Church that is not just predominantly a white one, but one that is almost totally identified with upper-middle-class values and aspirations.

The major question facing the Catholic Church everywhere in the world today is how to be catholic. The negative side of this challenge is the fear of breaking the unity of faith that must characterize the new world-Church. One senses that all are striving to articulate what that unity entails and how it is affected by the plurality of expressions that the divergent cultures demand. Such a tension does not in any way minimize the concern on the part of all for orthodoxy but sees that it is but one-half—at this moment, I suggest, the less difficult half—of the challenge.

In this context, the most important question that must be asked today is not what are the limits of unity, but what structures are best for this moment of history so that both the unity of belief and the plurality of cultural expression can be held together in that kind of creative tension that will bear fruit for the Church as it relates to the world. The world to which I refer here is not some abstract world, but our world of multicultural manifestations here and now.

Pope John XXIII raised these issues to a new level by calling Vatican Council II. But the Church was not yet ready to deal with them, because the experience of universalism, the experience of no longer being a western Church, the experience of relating to the world in a new way could only begin at and after that conciliar event. Although the documents of Vatican Council II seem to us to be its major product, the awareness of the Church's catholicity may turn out to be historically its most lasting effect.

UNIVERSAL STRUCTURES: SYNODS OF BISHOPS

Pope Paul VI tried to bring that awareness to the Church structures of his day by the internationalization of the Curia. The macropluralism of cultures would be reflected then in the micropluralism of the Curia. This important initiative, however, is not adequate to bring about the catholicity to which the council points. It would not be fair to expect that one could take people, however intelligent and goodwilled they may be, out of their culture and place them "as a minority" in another culture, and then demand that they continue to sustain a vital, living relationship with their native cultures—some of which are changing very rapidly. The odds are that they will be absorbed by the dominant culture and at the same time simply be out of touch with their own.

There is, instead, need for a central, multicultural point of unity that does not lose touch with the living cultures of which it is comprised. Such a structure, to respond to the demands of this moment of a nascent world-Church—that is, to maintain unity within a cultural pluralism—must have, first of all, a strong and dynamic point of unity. Fortunately that kind of papacy has been evolving since the middle of the last century. A weak center would end in a centrifugal dispersal that would be disastrous at this moment of pluralism and dilute any major influence of the Church in the world. A strong and morally influential papacy at this moment of history is an absolute requirement. It must be a papacy that holds together those forces that could become fissiparous and divisive. But it must also be a papacy that touches the farthest corners of the globe, that accepts the realism of being catholic, that creates a comprehensive and inclusive vision and prizes many levels of cooperative leadership.

Pope John Paul II has instinctively tried to respond to this new situation by his tireless and important trips around the world. In those trips he has attempted to articulate the points of unity, just as he has accepted much of the cultural pluralism. Not each trip has kept such a delicate balance, but I am sure that most of us have observed with admiration the significant achievements of these personal visits.

In sum, I would say that the major experience of Vatican Council II was not a new freedom or liberalism of doctrine, but a new demand for true universalism in all that affects Church life and mission. The old structures cannot support the new challenge of such a call to a fuller catholicity. The papal trips have kept alive the conciliar desire for it, but do not of themselves provide structures whereby it can become a reality.

The new structures that were designed to effect a deeper catholicity were two relatively new entities: the Roman Synods of Bishops and the local Conferences of Bishops.[3] They were considered to be vital in the search for universality in unity. Perhaps the greatest disappointment since Vatican Council II has been the breakdown of the effectiveness of these structures as vehicles of both unity and cultural diversity, communicating insights to the center from the local churches and from the center out to the local churches. The hope they engendered has, for the most part, not been realized.

The first of these two entities to become ineffective was the Roman Synod of Bishops. The first synods had begun to create a new atmosphere in the world-Church, where major decisions affecting the universal, culturally pluralistic Church would be weighed and discussed in just such a catholic atmosphere. The agenda of the Synods of 1967, 1969, and 1971 touched on many issues yet to be implemented after the council.[4] They tentatively took up the challenge of becoming a vital new structure that could remain close to the papacy and supply the needed catholic vision for the new age. The Roman Synod of 1971 was, in this sense, the most vigorous and most characteristic, as well as the greatest sign of hope for the future. Third-world nations—perhaps more spectators than actors at Vatican Council II—were alive and articulate in the Synod of 1971. The agenda touched their anticolonial search for a new freedom. The document on *Justice in the World* was a significant product of such strivings. The following synod (1974) on evangelization was also exciting in its multicultural search. However, by that time the varied agendas containing all the issues facing the world-Church were simply not presented to the members, and the synods were fast on their way to becoming simply useful international symposia. Three years, instead of two, would also lapse between synods. Having been a member of these early synods, I can attest to the hope they engendered.

In the intervening years since the mid-1970s the Curia has reasserted its former central role of trying to hold together the unity of the Church with its new cultural pluralism. In this new context the synods were seen as no longer needed or useful for continuous, ongoing contacts within a culturally pluralistic Church. To me it has seemed that subsequent synods have been interesting for the limited themes they have dealt with, but also have been frustrating, since they have never lasted long enough for the pluralism to surface and be articulated in a satisfying way. The input to these synods is much more interesting than the results, since the procedures only permit the articulation of least-common-denominator generalizations that—to fit the whole world—have been denuded of any cultural specificities. An enormous expectation level is raised by the preliminary preparations in each nation, but it is always diffused, since there is almost no follow-up after the document is finally published.

Thus the Roman Synods of Bishops do not provide the continuity needed for ongoing contacts between the center and the whole, nor among the culturally divergent local churches themselves.

Now is the time to rethink the aims of the synods and ask the basic question again: What should the synods be effecting for the Holy Father and for all the bishops, as the world-Church seeks to face the vital issues of our day? Can they become the Pope's sounding board and, thus, truly effective sources of collegiality with and for him, in seeing all the aspects of the world-Church today? Could there be a permanent synod that would meet yearly with representatives from various Conferences of Bishops, some — perhaps the officers of the conferences — being ex officio members, others being chosen because of the themes to be discussed? It certainly would not be more expensive than the many trips to Rome that some bishops must now make to attend *plenaria* of the various congregations and councils. Moreover, it would have the advantage that the members would be representative of the thinking of the various regions of the world. Finally, it would avoid the impression, true or false, that members of a *plenarium* are not appointed to give cultural pluralism but because of the conformity of their thinking.

One could envision various sub-synods within a major one to treat issues that affect specific areas of the world. So, for example, when I was chairing the committee writing the Economic Pastoral Letter of the U.S.A. bishops, I dreamt of meetings of U.S. bishops with Korean and Philippine bishops on the conditions of labor in their countries and the Church's doctrine on the rights of labor. Thus, we U.S. bishops could be of support to those areas of the globe where our nation has economic interests but the labor conditions are like those during the Industrial Revolution. Also appropriate would be meetings between U.S. and Central American bishops on human rights; meetings of U.S., German, Japanese, and Swiss bishops with third-world bishops on the third-world debt; meetings with many interested parties on Islamic and Jewish dialogues; and meetings of U.S. Black bishops with African bishops on liturgy. One could imagine an exciting scene where Rome could become central to the multicultural issues the world-Church faces.

THE NATIONAL CONFERENCES OF BISHOPS

The inner life of the Conferences of Bishops is also central to any world-Church today. It is where the Incarnation principle is seen at work and where the reflection and discernment of the action of the Spirit can and must take place. Unfortunately, the role of the conferences has been side-tracked by lengthy discussions of their teaching role and authority over against the particular church or diocese.[5] (It is curious that the role of provinces or archdioceses is not brought into the debate.) Common sense would indicate that if two hundred bishops agree on something about the faith, it carries more weight with listeners than if only one says it. Theologians must, of course, feel free to debate what that all means in terms of the teaching magisterium, but that discussion should not impede the growth of the conferences in order to fulfill other purposes.

Conferences are usually seen in one of two ways. First, they can be considered as mini or partial Ecumenical Councils. In this case the authority issue is paramount. All bishops, by reason of their ordination into the College of Bishops, are equal in such a context, and it would be difficult to see how there could be any restrictions on the roles of auxiliaries or retired. Second, these conferences can be seen as federations of particular churches or dioceses, each diocese being equal to the others in the conference. In this view, each local church would have one vote, it being cast by the diocesan bishop in the name of his particular church.[6] (Our conference acts in this manner only for matters concerning money!) Conferences are still a composite structure in evolution. Both aspects cited have some merit, but the latter has a special creative advantage. It could lead to exciting new developments with regard to the participation in the debates by other members of a local church, such as clergy and laity, even though the official vote would be cast by the diocesan bishop. This would be especially advantageous if and when the themes vitally touched the lives and competency of the clergy or laity.

Whatever structure one would develop, one should not neglect a third role: The utility of conferences for relating one sector of the Church to others and of being truly a sounding board for the Holy Father. There is no authentic role for a local conference in the world-Church if it is not tied into the role of primacy of the Pope. It is that bond which must be tightened and probed. The fact that the Holy Father spends so many hours in receiving bishops at their *ad limina* visits and met once, a few years ago, with the archbishops of the U.S.A., indicates that he understands the need today for effective solidarity with churches throughout the world and is looking for new structures to provide this kind of forum. Even without any preparation, the last meeting of the U.S. archbishops with the Pope and the Curia showed new possibilities for such contacts. A more formal structure, through the conferences, could make these meetings much more useful and fruitful.

This kind of bonding would also make cooperation among the conferences more feasible, especially when dealing with such difficult questions as war and peace, economic justice, ecology, ecumenism, and the role of women, to name but a few topics being dealt with by several conferences simultaneously. Such bonding would also prevent our own church in the U.S.A. from becoming too provincial. At this moment of history the church in the U.S.A. must face many crucial issues before other sectors of the world must do so; we thus need a world forum within the Church in which such discussion can take place on an international basis. It seems to me, too, that the question of the teaching authority of conferences would become a moot one, since conferences would not and could not be conceived of as standing alone, but always in solidarity with the Holy Father and with one another. Need I add what a fine model this would be for all the faithful as they seek to implement organs of collaboration on the diocesan and parochial levels?

ISSUES TO BE DISCUSSED

Once such structures were in place, what issues do I see as urgent for in-depth discussion and discernment? Any list will be incomplete, and every part of the world-Church would have a different set of issues and concerns of immediate importance. The following items are not listed according to a criterion of urgency, because all are urgent for our day.

1. It should be evident by now that the first item that must be examined is that of unity of belief in the midst of cultural pluralism. How far can one go in permitting various expressions of the same faith? How much of our faith tradition is bound up with western culture and has little to do with the gospel as preached by Jesus Christ? How can the new churches enrich the life of the older ones, and vice versa? How can those nations in the avant-garde of technology face up to the enormous ethical and moral questions now being posed, without leaving the other nations outside the dialogue? All of the challenges of becoming a world-Church arise in this context.

2. Regardless of where the Church finds itself on this globe, there will be certain questions about how the Church should engage the world in dialogue and debate. These Church–world issues will continue to challenge the People of God all over the entire planet. They range from life issues and human rights to freedom of religion and poverty. These major issues of our world today have taken on a new meaning with the startling events in Poland and throughout the Soviet bloc. These issues are calling out for critical clarification in the light of our faith tradition. They are tied into our concepts of democracy, the liberalism of the Enlightenment, the role of government, private property, ecology, and a host of other connected questions. Catholic social teaching has much to say about these issues. Now is the moment to look at them again from the perspective of our world today in its striking evolution toward a new mode of international political relationships.

3. Are we ready to look anew at the challenge of the role of women in Church and society on an international level? It is not, as the Roman Synod of Bishops of 1987 (on the role of laity in the world) proved, a question restricted to the U.S.A., but one that affects the whole world. Are we able to look at it positively? What psychological fears must first be dealt with? The future of the Church in countries such as the U.S.A. depends on the

answer we give to that question. We cannot permit another generation to grow up in the Church with the negative feelings that are now found there. Women have been vital to the history of our Church; they must continue to be so and not become alienated and frustrated.

4. Of the internal problems facing the Church, the most pressing is that of sacramental practice—the priesthood and lay ministry. With the reduction of the number of clergy in some areas of the world, the question is constantly posed: Will we slowly become a Church of the Word only? Have we created such a thirst for a eucharistic community among our people that they will not accept anything that seems to be an ersatz? The experiences in my own diocese show that people want to dialogue on a broader basis about how they can keep their Church a center of sacramental life and not be reduced to the image of another Protestant Church of the Word only.[7]

5. What ecumenical breakthrough does the Spirit seem to be leading us to? What signs are there of hope in this area? There can be no "Catholic moment" if it is separated from our ties with those churches we have been in intense dialogue with for these past twenty-five years. The breakup of the Soviet Union has opened up new opportunities in this respect, and they must be taken advantage of. The negative spirit that has crept into the minds of many with regard to ecumenism must be dispelled.

6. What contribution should we be making as Church to the ethical and moral issues that are at the forefront of our society today? These issues touch everything from ecological to bioethical and medical questions of prime importance, through AIDS, to Wall Street scandals. The agenda is without end, and the need for continual rational discourse is also infinite. There is, as well, a need in this regard to use the sociological and psychological tools at our disposal for an accurate understanding of existing realities. The current skepticism, or even animosity, toward these human sciences deprives the Church of much-needed insights, since they act as a strong corrective to easy a priori solutions that do not correspond to the real needs.

7. There is also a need to examine internal-justice issues within the Church. If not, then our witness to these values as we speak to the world will become very clouded.

8. Lastly, in this succinct list, I would like to mention lay and clerical spirituality. All people crave insights that would help them lead virtuous lives under the pressures of the culture they live in, develop a deeper personal prayer life, probe more scientifically, but prayerfully, into scripture and liturgy. They are seeking inspirations that would lead them into more concrete action for the poor and needy. In other words, they are seeking how to lead holy lives in a world that does not prize such holiness. They are seeking a personal vision of holiness within the broader Church commitment and a personal way to become a part of what it means to be "Sacrament to the world."

There are many other items that could be added to this list: the future, role, and content of Catholic education; mass media and culture; religious freedom and suffering; ecology and the use of the goods of this earth for the benefit of all; religious life. The list could be endless.

URGENCY OF THE MOMENT

Pope John XXIII, in *Pacem in terris*, pointed out the significant signs of our times. He lamented the fact that there was no international structure that could deal with all of the vital issues of a new global society. The trend in the world toward mutual interdependency, recognized so clearly by him, will continue to grow, not decrease, in the next century. The U.S.A. lies at the center of such growth, although it will never assume again the role of hegemony that it once felt it enjoyed. Nevertheless, its role is and will remain central to the life of the whole world. The Church shares the vision of mutual interdependency. It already admits this quality is essential to its nature and has gained an international catholic presence. We in the U.S.A. should be among the first in the Church to welcome, support, and delineate those structures needed for a world-Church to exist and function well. Isolationism as an ecclesiology makes no sense at all.

We also should be among the first to assist the Holy Father to play that role of point of unity and orthodoxy that is so crucial to the world-Church and, by our candor and sincerity, try to bring forth the issues that challenge us and the world. The vision we all need at this moment of world history is a world vision. It would be a shame and a shirking of duty if we permitted our energies and hopes to be sapped by useless debates on nonessentials and internal bickerings that create a climate of distrust, discouragement, and depression — certainly not a sign of what God has in mind for the world.

A moment of grace is upon us. We must respond to the promptings of the Spirit and become, not just in words but truly in fact, a world-Church — in our thinking and attitudes, in our structures, in our actions and deeds. At the same time we must strive in the local church to be vital, welcoming places where people can find the transcendent in liturgy and life and the kind of supportive community described in the Acts of the Apostles as existing in Jerusalem — a characteristic that should be true of all communities of disciples of Christ.

CHAPTER 3

The Kingdom of God
and This World

The Unfinished Symphony

When Tadeusz Mazowiecki, after becoming the first premier of the new free Poland in August 1989, was interviewed by western correspondents, he stated that the principles that would guide the new regime in this first postcommunist state would be Catholic social teaching—a statement much quoted around the world.[1] Newspapers and columnists from various parts of the U.S.A. phoned me to find out, in one or two succinct sentences, what this teaching was all about. Although it had been clearly a part of Catholic consciousness for over a hundred years, having been formally stated as such by Pope Leo XIII in his social encyclical *Rerum novarum* of 1891, one could not say that in the mind of the American public, even among Catholics, it had become a household term. But Mazowiecki was not the first to mention that body of teaching as an inspiration for modern government. One could also cite the writings and speeches of De Gasperi, Schuman, Adenauer, and so many of the post-World War II Catholic political leaders and founders of the Christian Democratic parties of Europe and show how they were inspired by Catholic social teaching. One cannot understand how the Church around the world today seeks to relate to state and society without knowing the basis of this teaching.

Moreover, the pontificate of Pope John Paul II will be seen by historians, decades from now, as having brought to the fore again the Church's social teaching. Although previous Popes, especially Pope John XXIII and Pope Paul VI, also contributed much to this body of teaching, the writings and speeches of the present Pope in the area of social doctrine have been more extensive and more innovative.[2] Moreover, he has had the opportunity of preaching these teachings around the globe and thus of applying them to concrete circumstances. In the third world and countries in the middle of material development, these teachings have been well accepted, even considered by many there as prophetic. In the first world, however, they have not met with the same enthusiasm, especially among the neoconservative Catholic political groups and those Catholics in the higher ranks of business. In reiterating these teachings, however, one could say that the present Pope is a true successor of Vatican Council II, especially if one sees such documents as *The Church in the Modern World* as indicative of the new role the Church should play in the affairs of this world.

But Catholic social teaching did not begin with Vatican Council II. It is a rather unsystematic body of ideas that grew up in the last hundred years as a response to some of the urgent social questions of our day. Vatican Council II made this trend "official," as it were, and laid the theological foundation for subsequent teaching. Since Catholic social teaching is not a body of complete and coherent doctrine, I have dubbed it "The Unfinished Symphony," with the understanding that it is constantly being composed as the Church moves to new challenges in its interfacing with the world. It would be helpful to reflect on that teaching and how it grew up in the last hundred years, on its basic contents as found in Vatican Council II and papal documents, on its theological underpinnings, and on its normative value as Catholic teaching.

GROWTH THROUGH EXPERIENCE

It would be false to think that the Church only began to reflect on how it relates to this world with the encyclical *Rerum novarum* of Pope Leo XIII in 1891. That question was asked in biblical times and throughout history. Those answers through history always tried to keep a balance between the vicissitudes of this world and the inevitability of the world to come. The perspective was more eschatological than in our own day; people looked more to the end of the world than to the social arrangements of this world. The concept of a social "problem" that faith had something to say to is more a product of our own times. In fact, one could say that the Church in the past seemed reluctant to enter into questions such as slavery, poverty, dictatorships, and the like because they were a part of the worldview that all accepted. This medieval construct was brought to an end, however, with the Enlightenment and the revolutions of the eighteenth century. A new mode of seeing the human person and society evolved. As a result the Church was forced to reflect on these new configurations, and do so in a new way. The end of feudalism also provoked fresh thinking on the part of the Church.

It would also be wrong to assume that *Rerum novarum*, coming as it does at the beginning of the last decade of the century, is an original and pioneering work. It was preceded by many lay movements within the Church, and profited immeasurably from them.[3] The initial Catholic response to the Industrial Revolution was slow, but it gained momentum as the century progressed. Pope Leo XIII took advantage of that momentum, and thus his writings are the culmination of a period, not the beginning.

Nevertheless, *Rerum novarum*, and, as we will see, so much of Catholic social teaching, was a reaction to the conditions of the times. It was, one could say, the official response to the conditions induced by the Industrial Revolution. Its teachings were a reaction to forces in society that Leo felt were inimical to the Church and to the well-being of its faithful.

Leo's insistence on the rights of private property was not based so much on the desire to support the philosophical teachings of Enlightenment philosophers but on the need for a way of combating Communism—viewed as a new religion, a new human community that was in opposition to religion. Nor is that encyclical a complete exposition of human rights or a theological teaching on the source of such rights; it is rather a strong insistence on private property as the way in which God wanted humans to use this earth. Leo saw that he was taking sides on an issue that was highly political, but felt that he had to do so to protect the faithful from a false ideology.

His teachings on the rights of workers were also very much in response to the abuses of the times. He had no alternative but to condemn the unhealthy and inhuman working conditions brought on by the Industrial Revolution. To balance these negative trends, he supported the rights that workers have to form associations and unions in order to protect their interests. These affirmations were the beginnings of the concept of human dignity that was to pervade so much of subsequent Catholic social teaching. Thus, although Leo was reacting to the abuses of the times, he was also creating the bases for much later teaching on human dignity and human rights.

Forty years later his successor, Pope Pius XI, in his encyclical *Quadragesimo anno* (1931), added to this teaching, while reiterating the same basic doctrines of his predecessor. The growth in the concepts were again forced by new circumstances. The "statism" arising in Germany and Italy prompted the Pope to speak out in favor of "subsidiarity," the need for the state to help or aid the local level to take responsibility for those social concerns that properly touched them.[4] Although the role of the state was seen as positive, it was also seen as limited. Subsidiarity became the new and important concept in Catholic social teaching, one much favored by the laity, because it meant a positive delegation to the lower level and prevented the higher authority from assuming too much power. Subsidiarity gave birth to many fruitful concepts of human endeavor, especially in the economic field, that were smaller and more manageable. Often it was paraphrased as "Small is beautiful," although this was not its original intent. It is a principle that tries to control an ever greater tendency toward centralization. The debate whether this principle is also applicable to the Church has stirred emotional responses. Pope Pius XII said yes to that question. Today the debate continues, with Cardinal Ratzinger on the negative side and Cardinal Hume of Westminster on the positive.[5]

There seems to be a long gap between the encyclical of Pope Pius XI, *Quadragesimo anno* (1931), and the social encyclicals of Pope John XXIII. There is not, however, a gap in ideas. In his later writings Pope Pius XI began to make the human person the fundamental reference point of his social teaching. Pope Pius XII, in his Christmas messages — although they were not encyclicals — reiterated the main thrust and teachings of the Church on social teaching, kept it alive, and applied it to current situations. The Church was not unaffected by the forces that led up to the Universal Declaration of Human Rights in 1948, but did not really make that concept its own until the teachings of Pope John XXIII in his famous encyclicals *Mater et Magistra* (1961) and *Pacem in terris* (1963).

The concepts of human dignity and human rights that flow from that dignity characterized the teaching of Pope John. His list of those rights in *Pacem in terris* has been used as a basis for further elaboration through time. One could add as a second and no less important contribution by this Pope his intuitive sense that Catholic social teaching must face up to the new global situation the world found itself in. If Pope Pius XI saw the value of subsidiarity and delegation of power to the local level, Pope John saw the need to complement this with a sense of the well-being of the whole world, stating that there were some issues that could only be treated now in a global way. Since his time, that tendency has grown ever more evident. He lamented the lack of international bodies to deal with these rising global concerns. The economic thrust since his time has shown how correct he was. Our ecological concerns point in the same direction.

Pope Paul VI focused his attention in another direction, one that has very much influenced Pope John Paul II. In his writings, such as the encyclical *Populorum progressio* (1967) and the apostolic letter *Octogesima adveniens* (1971), Pope Paul brought forward for consideration the growing economic gap between the north and the south, the first and the third worlds. With these documents the Pope came to loggerheads with the neo-conservative movement in the U.S.A. Much of his writings blame the first world for the disparities in wealth and wealth distribution in the world. Pope Paul's writings were highly influenced by the vision of the *Church in the Modern World* of Vatican Council II and were an attempt to make that vision more explicit. There is an urgency of tone to his writings, and many have noted that they seem to have a more socialist tinge than the work of his predecessors.

The present pontificate will go down in history as one that has emphasized the social teaching of the Church. Pope John Paul II began this influence with his first encyclical, *Redemptor hominis* (1979). He places Christ at the center of all his teaching, including that of social doctrine. Although much of his thought is philosophically inspired, he returns frequently to Christ as the focal point of all history. Three encyclicals dealing with social teaching have marked his pontificate: *Laborem exercens* (1981), *Sollicitudo rei socialis* (1987), and *Centesimus annus* (1991). The first of these is indeed an original document, bringing up-to-date much of the thinking of Pope Leo XIII on labor. New terminology is introduced, but the concepts remain the same. Because of his experience of living under Marxist regimes, the present Pope is able to be very concrete in his analysis of the rights of labor. Some did not find there a complete analysis of what has happened to labor in the first world, but his teaching certainly was important for the forming and supporting of the labor movements that brought about such a remarkable change in the socialist countries.

Sollicitudo rei socialis is a remarkably strong document, reiterating all the preoccupations of Pope Paul VI concerning the disparities between the third world and the industrialized nations. It is a poignant cry for more equity in the distribution of the world's goods. *Centesimus annus* marks the hundredth anniversary of the first social encyclical by Pope Leo XIII and brings up-to-date the teaching contained in the historic document. In some senses it is able to leave behind those elements of that teaching that are no longer relevant. More than anything else, written as it was right after the demise of Marxism in the Eastern European bloc, it remains a historic analysis of that fall and at the same time a plea for a more equitable and humane capitalism.

SUMMARY OF CATHOLIC SOCIAL TEACHING

Because of the historical context of all the papal encyclicals, and because of the large range of topics dealt with and the lack of a single document that tries to sum up the whole, it is not easy to summarize Catholic social teaching. I will use here two very different sources to show the range of teaching and the topics dealt with. My first source is a listing by Michael J. Schultheis, Edward P. Berri, and Peter J. Henriot in the well-known and useful manual called *Our Best Kept Secret.*[6] The authors name, in chapter 4, fourteen major themes found in that teaching. I will cite their listing with some comments of my own.

1. *Link of religious and social dimensions of life.* This observation has been alluded to before. It means that Catholic social teaching believes that faith should influence how we act and what kind of society we desire to construct. It says something about right relationships between God and us and among ourselves.

2. *Dignity of the human person.* Probably no other value in Catholic social teaching has become so apparent as this one in the teaching of Vatican Council II. It permeates the thinking of that council and has marked the policies of the Church since then. It explains the Church's deep involvement in the pro-life movement and all those policies that favor the advancement of persons so they can live dignified lives. It also underlies the Church's position on many issues that involve labor.

3. *Political and economic rights.* Rights language is late in Catholic social teaching and is important for its inclusion of economic rights as well. Such

rights are intimately tied into the role of the dignity of each person. But such rights must be lived out in community.

4. *Option for the poor.* Because of the previous value, this one naturally follows. Those who are marginalized in society need special attention. The American bishops did not hesitate to call this value the touchstone of any economic system: how well it supports the dignity of the poor. It is also very easy to validate this value in both the Hebrew scriptures and in the New Testament.

5. *Link of love and justice.* Charity is always a part of the Christian proclamation of the gospel. On the other hand, although every disciple is called to such charity, it is not seen as a solution to injustice in the society. Other means are necessary to rectify those injustices that prevent some from sharing fully in the goods of society.

6. *Promotion of the common good.* Catholic social teaching has always admitted a tension between the rights of the individual and the needs of the society as such. It has always held to the value of the common good, in spite of the many times this was wrongly interpreted to mean the Church supported a socialist or even collectivist position. It has been the merit of the Church in its social teaching to hold up both values and to see that one cannot be validly maintained without the other, regardless of the difficulties involved in maintaining both.

7. *Subsidiarity.* This principle, enunciated by Pope Pius XI, stipulates that the state should assist those at lower levels to take the responsibility for the decisions that belong to them. It avoids undue centralization and permits the growth of mediating structures in society.

8. *Political participation.* The Church has had a positive view of government and thus of the duty of each citizen to participate in that government. In this respect, the Church has softened its position on democracy with the years, no longer seeing it as identifying the will of God with a majority of the people. It also becomes a necessary means for the promotion of the common good.

9. *Economic justice.* The Church has broadened its concept of justice to include also the rights of all to share in this earth's goods. In that equation, the rights of the person (labor) are more important than capital. In this area the Church has evolved rather developed thinking about labor and its rights, as well.

10. *Stewardship.* One could say that this is a latecomer in Catholic social teaching. More recent documents have made the ecological issues a priority. Nevertheless, there is a tension between the anthropocentric view cited earlier, when the value of the dignity of the person was spoken of, and the ecological perspective, which tends to broaden the concern. I expect that this tension will be the subject of much debate in the Catholic community in the decades to come.

11. *Global solidarity.* Beginning with the encyclicals of Pope John XXIII, this perception has become a centerpiece for almost all subsequent reflec-

tions. The global nature of our economy has emphasized the urgency of keeping in mind the new global dimension of almost every issue. Catholic social teaching in the last decades has repeatedly brought out the disparity of wealth among the various sectors of this world, especially between the northern and the southern part of the hemispheres.

12. *Promotion of peace.* The theme of peace as a justice issue is a good one that is reiterated in Catholic social teaching, especially in more recent times. Pope Paul VI connected the two when he changed the old Roman proverb to say: If you want peace, work for justice. He was consistent in pointing out that the roots of war lie in injustice among peoples.

13. *Work.* Much of the earlier Catholic social teaching dealt with this category of concerns. At the beginning it was more directed against abuses. In the writings of Pope John Paul II, it becomes more integrated in a positive fashion into the whole theory of the human person and how work relates to the development of that person.

14. *Liberation.* This word is somewhat new in Catholic social teaching and finds its origins in Latin American thought. It was then picked up by Vatican documents in an attempt to give it a meaning that would be consistent with Catholic social tradition and avoid ambiguities. It highlights the need to look at social structures that hamper the full development of the person.

To this list one could add the insights of two scholars, George E. McCarthy and Royal W. Rhodes, in their significant book, *Eclipse of Justice.*[7] They also mention the concern for the poor and powerless, as well as the stress on the dignity of the person. They add to the latter—and rightly—the full range of rights that flow from that dignity—political, economic, and social. They list separately the right to private property as a natural safeguard of personal dignity and freedom. This must be added because of the significant role that right has played in the history of Catholic social teaching since the time of Pope Leo XIII. They also mention the Church's defense of its right to apply social morality to social, political, and economic affairs. They list separately the Church's lengthy teaching on labor and its rights, including the right of organization and association and the right to strike, although the latter was slower in evolving. They continue on to talk about the expanded teaching of the present Pope that labor has a right to participate in decisions that affect its well-being.

They note that capital is viewed in different ways in agrarian and industrial contexts, but also note the teaching of the present Pope on the priority of labor. They also note the Church's positive assessment of the role of government and its right to intervene for the common good. They note as well the startling reversal of historical stereotypes, in that the Catholic Church is now often seen as the strongest opposition to oppressive regimes. One important point that is mentioned is the Church's eschewing of all ideologies in an attempt to remain faithful to the gospel and its support of the dignity of the person. Lastly, they emphasize the new internationalization of the overview given to social teaching.

THEOLOGICAL UNDERPINNINGS

The theoretical question remains: How does the Kingdom of God relate to this world here and now? Where can the Kingdom of God be found now?

In response to that question, theologians throughout history have brought up many different responses. During the Patristic period, because the Church was being so violently persecuted, the end-times seemed near; the fulfillment of the Kingdom seemed at hand. Thus the above question did not seem to be an urgent one that had to be asked. The fulfillment of the Kingdom was not far away; one prayed for perseverance and fidelity. After the peace of Constantine, the situation changed for the Church. It became necessary to ask that question in all earnestness. The end of time seemed postponed indefinitely. Although we live in the in-between times and await the second coming of our Savior Jesus Christ, what is our relationship to what is happening in this world in this time of expectation? Is there some relationship between what we do in the here and now and the end-time, or the fulfillment of the Kingdom?

The answer given then by so many theologians seemed to be sufficient for centuries. Basing their thinking mostly on the Gospel of St. John, theologians constructed a kind of dualism. Thus, Eusebius of Caesarea was able to see in the reign of Constantine the messianic fulfillment. All opposition would be considered the reign of evil. In the west, most often this position is associated with interpretations of the thinking and writings of St. Augustine, but it should probably be more aligned with that of Marcion. Augustine spoke, it is true, of two cities: the *civitas Dei* and the *civitas terrena*, but this division is not to be simply equated with the Church vis-à-vis the state, nor the Kingdom of Evil over against the Kingdom of God or the Church. The line of division cuts across as aspects of society and the Church.[8] Luther, however, basing his analysis on Augustine, was later to use this symbolism for his own *Zwei Reiche* theory, which has deep Johannine roots and is the basis for almost all apocalyptic literature. A battle between the forces of good and evil is always self-evident in such apocalyptic writings. For the faithful and their leaders, it is only one step, then, to project this dichotomy into actual situations they find themselves in and then very naturally to identify who is on the side of God and who is on the side of Satan or evil.

The Platonic roots of this neat distinction did not last into the high Middle Ages, and thus Aquinas was able to color this theory with his concept that the supernatural does not do away with, but completes, the natural. The dualism thus becomes blurred.

In the Marcion interpretation, the Kingdom of God is so easily conceived of spatially. It does not square well with the parables in Matthew's Gospel, where the Kingdom is likened to yeast in the dough or a seed that grows into a large tree or a field with both wheat and weeds that will be separated only in the harvest. But it is an enticing thesis and has persisted into our own day. Some still fall back on it for its simplicity. It also seems to satisfy psychological profiles of certain Christians who tend to see everything as black or white.

In the Catholic Church, some fall into this spatial definition when they identify the Kingdom of God with the Catholic Church. Walter Kasper has expressed this fallacy clearly: "The Church is only an effective and accomplished sacramental sign, not the reality of the Kingdom of God itself."[9] Anything outside the Catholic Church is looked upon with suspicion when such an identification takes place. Such a clear dualism makes ecumenism impossible. Such a thesis also tends to see the Church as the perfect society—a kind of realized eschatology. It then becomes the mission of the Church to expand and embrace everything and everyone. The state must be "catholicized." In this view, the ultimate fulfillment of the Kingdom will come when all have converted to Catholicism. Many might not say that thesis so bluntly, but it is contained in their hypotheses.

Among Protestants this thesis is especially attractive to Fundamentalists and Evangelicals. There one finds a tendency to label those "saved" as belonging to the Kingdom of God and all the others as being in that of the Devil. They interpret everything that happens in the world in terms of the combat between the two kingdoms. Here the state, too, must be christianized, so it can play a major messianic role in spreading the gospel. Jerry Falwell often writes in this vein when he describes the role that the U.S.A. must play in the mission of evangelization.

But Vatican Council II had a different perspective. To avoid the simple and easy identification of the Kingdom of God with the Catholic Church, they spoke of the Kingdom of God "subsisting in" the Church. This phrase has been the subject of much debate these days, but the phrase and the discussion around it during the council make no sense if it were just a question of identification. The Holy Spirit can work outside the Church, even if we believe that the Church is the instrument of the Kingdom and that one can be certain that the means of salvation are to be found within the Church. In this model of Vatican II, the Holy Spirit is seen as ahead of the Church, as if pulling it on to the greater good of the Kingdom. Recognizing the signs of the times, or how the Spirit is functioning out in the world, is a part of the discerning process that the Church must be constantly engaged in.

This model seems to correspond better to the parables about the Kingdom in the gospel. The kingdoms of good and evil are not spatially separated but found in every aspect of life. They are found in the person because of original sin; they are found in society; they are found in government; they are found in the Church—*semper reformanda*. This model of interpenetrability as the document *Gaudium et spes* called it, corresponds best to the images of the gospel and to the reality we all have experienced.

Pope John Paul II is quite clear and precise in rejecting this dualistic interpretation, and does so in striking terms:

> But no political society—which possesses its own autonomy and laws—can ever be confused with the Kingdom of God. The Gospel parable of the weeds among the wheat (cf. Matthew 13:24–30; 36–43) teaches that it is for God alone to separate the subjects of the Kingdom from the subjects of the Evil One, and that this judgment will take place at the end of time. By presuming to anticipate judgment here and now, man puts himself in the place of God and sets himself against the patience of God.[10]

Our culture has come to know another extreme with regard to how the Kingdom of God relates to this world. This temptation is to reduce the Kingdom of God to a spiritual one. It is part of modernity, since the time of the Enlightenment, to consider religion as personal or private, dealing with the person's conscience—that there is nothing objective in religion because it cannot be studied under a microscope in a scientific fashion or subjected to purely rational processes. Religion cannot be measured. The result of this vision of religion is to reduce the role of the Church to that of "saving souls," or a spiritual mission.

Because of this new dualism in which religion has been reduced to the spiritual, it does not have anything to say to the secular world. In some respects this becomes the old division into the profane and the sacred. It would seem that the world then can be easily divided between those areas that are secular and those that are religious. The Church would have nothing to say about the secular; it simply would lack competence in that area. Politics and social issues are usually thus defined as secular. The Church must stay out of politics, according to such a view. Often to reinforce this dualism, the Enlightenment idea of the wall between Church and state is brought forth, interpreting this separation not in its original sense that no Church should be the preferred religion of the state, but that political and often societal issues do not have religious or moral content.

This crass separation is seldom found now in public debates, but it was still around in force but a decade ago. It seems to be dying slowly, as our present generation is seeing that politics and business do involve ethical and moral issues that are also the purview of religion. From a gospel point of view, one could not imagine that God set aside some areas where the Divine presence could not or would not penetrate—a sacred secular preserve. The principle of the Incarnation is precisely that God becomes one of us, taking on the whole of the human condition. Paul makes it clear that the whole of creation is affected by that Incarnation and seeks its unity and ultimate harmony through the mediation of Jesus Christ. The passages where he speaks of the "cosmic" Christ show that the Kingdom of God potentially embraces the whole world. No aspect of it is outside God's love and care.

NORMATIVE VALUE OF CATHOLIC SOCIAL TEACHING

Some in our day assert that, as one looks at the body of all that the Church teaches, one can reject Catholic social teaching because it is optional, that is, not an essential part of the gospel message. Such an opinion grew up in the U.S.A. during the 1960s when some Catholic intellectuals here were disturbed by the social teaching of Pope John XXIII in his encyclicals *Mater et Magistra* (1961) and *Pacem in terris* (1963). The debate continued during that decade and into the Synod of Bishops in 1971, when the theme of *Justice in the World* was discussed. The assembled bishops settled on the following often-quoted sentence:

Action on behalf of justice and participation in the transformation of the world fully appear to us as a constitutive dimension of the preaching of the gospel, or, in other words, of the Church's mission for the redemption of the human race and its liberation from every oppressive situation.[11]

This sentence was still not accepted by many because they asserted that *Justice in the Modern World* was never approved officially by Pope Paul VI. To the dismay of some, I am sure, the debate is now ended—at least for those who accept papal teaching as normative. In his recent encyclical, *Centesimus annus*, Pope John Paul II, discussing the hundredth anniversary of Pope Leo XIII's first social encyclical, *Rerum novarum*, wrote:

To spread her social doctrine pertains to the Church's evangelizing mission and is an essential part of the Christian message, since this doctrine points out the direct consequences of that message in the life of society and situates daily work and struggles for justice in the context of bearing witness to Christ the Savior.[12]

The word *essential*, fought for by many bishops at the Synod of 1971 but voted down, is certainly stronger than the term *constitutive*. All of us must now wrestle with that body of social teaching, ferret out its biblical roots, struggle to understand its natural-law philosophical underpinnings, and worry about its correct application to our lives and history today.

Although the doctrine itself is declared essential to the full message of the Church, it must be clearly affirmed that the Church places more weight on the principles of its teaching than on each application thereof. In other words, it asserts that the principles are indeed true, but that in the application, as one moves from the theoretical to the concrete, the degree of certitude becomes less weighty. One is never in control of all the factors involved in the analysis of a situation, and people can rightly disagree on such an interpretation of facts. In the pastoral letter *Economic Justice for All*, the bishops make this distinction:

> Our judgments and recommendations on specific economic issues, therefore, do not carry the same moral authority as our statements of universal moral principles and formal church teaching; the former are related to circumstances which can change or which can be inter-preted differently by people of good will. We expect and welcome debate on our specific policy recommendations. Nevertheless, we want our statements on these matters to be given serious consideration by Catholics as they determine whether their own moral judgments are consistent with the Gospel and with Catholic social teaching. We believe that differences on complex economic questions should be expressed in a spirit of mutual respect and open dialogue.[13]

Pope John Paul II makes similar disavowals in the introduction to his last encyclical, *Centesimus annus*. He writes:

> The present Encyclical seeks to show the fruitfulness of the principles enunciated by Leo XIII, which belong to the Church's doctrinal pat-rimony and, as such, involve the exercise of her teaching authority. But pastoral solicitude also prompts me to propose an analysis of some events of recent history. It goes without saying that part of the responsibility of Pastors is to give careful consideration to current events in order to discern the new requirements of evangelization. However, such an analysis is not meant to pass definitive judgments since this does not fall per se within the Magisterium's specific domain.[14]

These distinctions may at first seem subtle, but they are very practical and useful as one attempts to apply the social principles of the Church to concrete cases and actions. There the Church admits a certain amount of ambiguity in the light of the analysis one makes of the case at hand.

It has been mentioned that Catholic social teaching has continued to grow for a century now. It is expected that it will continue to do so. The new ecological issues demand a rethinking about the limits of this earth and the care we must extend to it. The relationship between the human person and this earth also will need more reflection. The whole question of labor and its application in an international economy is far from finished. There is but one short phrase about the role of women in today's economy in the encyclical *Centesimus annus*, but that theme will be uppermost in our minds in the next decade. At the same time, there is a desire to wed the natural-law tradition and the biblical, so that the basis of Catholic social tradition is clear and the demands of discipleship are cogent. The growth process, as one can see, is far from finished.

PART II

RELIGION AND THE PUBLIC FORUM

INTRODUCTION

For a Catholic, no area of contemporary life is as complicated as that of the relationship between faith and politics. The older model of a state religion seemed easier than our current democratic one that involves separation of Church and state and a resultant pluralism, one that seems to cause confusion and sometimes chaos. Catholicism must now function in societies that are not Catholic and where Catholicism has and seeks no preferential role. Although this pluralism has been theoretically accepted by the documents of Vatican Council II, a clear modus operandi for Catholics has not been thought out. At the synod on the laity in 1987, it was evident from the descriptions given that the situation varies so much throughout the world that no common guideline could be laid down. In some African nations, for example, Catholics are a small minority in a predominantly Muslim culture; in other areas of the globe Catholicism is the dominant religion in the nation; in many countries, such as our own, it is one of many religions—large, but not the dominant factor. Each situation demands a different reflection and solution. My concern in this section is for the Catholic politician in the U.S.A. today.

The situation was easier for Catholics when they were the outsiders in American culture and not engaged so deeply in the political life of the nation. Now they must confront the situation more clearly. Often rational discourse and reasoning is not possible because Catholics find themselves in positions where rapid decisions affecting political careers must be made without the leisure for lengthy dialogue. Although Catholics were encouraged to enter politics and play their role fully in American society, they may well think twice about doing so if they feel that the hierarchy will always be standing behind them to see if they are voting consistently according to Catholic norms.

Because of these difficulties, there are new mine fields out there that

43

seem to trap either the clergy or the politician and are grounds for often bitter tensions between clergy and laity.

A new question that also must be asked, now that the Catholic religion is the largest single religious body in U.S. society, is the role in the political process, not of the individual Catholic acting alone, but of the Church as such—hierarchy and laity acting together. The response one gives to this issue affects parish life as well. For what causes should the parishioners be mobilized in order to effect social and legislative change? We have not hesitated to do so when the cause affected us Catholics or our school systems, that is, when it was an inner Catholic cause, such as school busing or textbooks. We have not hesitated to do so when we felt the issue at stake was one of life or death, such as the decisions that affect abortion. In the case of war, however, we seem to be very divided. Note the reactions even among the hierarchy in support of the Gulf war, in spite of the clear and unambiguous speeches of the Holy Father taking a contrary position. We are less motivated to enter the fray as a Church body, however, if there is no self-interest or if the issue is capital punishment, welfare, or any of the more divisive human concerns. On almost all such issues we tend to leave each individual free to make his or her own decision, hiding behind the wall of separation of Church and state to defend such individual freedom.

One aspect of this issue that has not been thoroughly discussed consists of an analysis of the relationship between the convictions of the elected official and the sentiments of the constituency represented. If there is a conflict between the personal beliefs of the elected official and the majority of the constituents, how should such a situation be handled? One would not automatically say that the politician should resign. It could well be that a deep conflict would result in such a resignation, but one would hope that some kind of compromise could be reached. How deep can such a compromise go? Can a Catholic, in other words, be a candidate for a district in which the majority of the voters are pro-choice in the issue of abortion? In this regard, we all have come to accept in the U.S. scene today that a candidate for office often takes a position to be elected but then flip-flops after election. We are so accustomed to this maneuver that we do not put too much faith in what candidates say. We look at other aspects of their personality. How serious should we take the preelection positions of a candidate? Are they strategies or convictions?

Vatican II expects the laity to be the instrument of evangelization to the public square. How will the Church encourage its laity to work to transform American culture—to evangelize it, as the current language would say? Is the Church saying that we will live now with the pluralism of U.S. culture, but secretly our aim is to make everyone Catholic, to evangelize the nation? What are our ultimate aims as a Church? Have they been clearly articulated? If we win the abortion issue, what is the next one we will tackle? There is some fear in the general public, some residue of the old anti-Catholicism, so these questions are posed to us in private but not discussed in public.

A further tension exists between the laity and the hierarchy or clergy with regard to societal and political issues. One solution could be called the German model, since it seems to dominate the way in which the German Conference of Bishops relates to the lay political component. That model suggests that it is the role of the hierarchy and clergy to express the the-oretical or theological doctrine behind a political or societal issue, but to leave to the laity the actual formulation of the needed legislative action. In that model the bishops do not suggest any concrete action; they do not descend to the details but remain on the level of principles, that is, they teach the doctrine involved in the issue at hand. But the distinction between the theory and its implementation is not always an easy one to make in concrete situations. Often, too, there is the suspicion that the clergy are secretly pulling the strings behind the scenes, making the laity into puppets.

There is an added sensitivity among Catholics in the U.S.A. to political issues, especially if discussed from the pulpit by the clergy. They resent the clergy telling them how to vote and how to respond to questions that they feel are their private responsibility. Too much pressure on the part of the hierarchy or clergy usually produces the opposite of the effect intended.

One should also mention the need to broaden this discourse to include the ecumenical community. So often a church finds itself in alliance with other churches to effect the common good of all. These actions can easily take on political overtones and often even lead to direct affirmative action. Such collaborative efforts are encouraged, but at times the Catholic position will not correspond with that of its partners. Nevertheless such coalitions are important today in order to effect a better society.

These problems seem exacerbated in the political realm because they receive there much notice and importance. But similar questions could be asked about the role of Catholics in business, in the arts, in communications and the media. It is a shame that we have restricted the issues too much to the political arena.

The three essays in this section deal with some of these issues. I realize the tentativeness of so much of this discourse and the need to deepen the debate on all the questions raised thus far. One could say that the three next chapters wrestle with some of the dilemmas connected with being insiders in our culture. We hold strong convictions as Catholics on many issues, but at the same time, we find ourselves perhaps unwilling to elimi-nate the pluralism that characterizes that culture, because we have found such pluralism so beneficial. The first article is more specifically concerned with the models of how religion and society relate. It shows the many models that have historically existed and how they have changed through the thinking of Vatican Council II. The second deals with the tension between laity and clergy over ways of influencing this world. The third is more specific in nature and seeks to encourage Catholics, in spite of the many difficulties involved, to continue to take their place in politics and public life.

CHAPTER 4

Religion and Public Policy

For a discussion on the role of the lay Catholic politician, let me begin with a scenario.[1] On the first Sunday of Advent in 1983, Mario Cuomo, Governor of the State of New York, who also happens to be a Catholic, spoke at the Episcopal Cathedral of St. John the Divine in the city of New York. I had to admit that the dilemma he posed resonated with my own experience, and I sympathized with him in having to solve it, since I as a bishop had been asked by Catholic politicians to reflect with them on the same issue. The governor at that time had to wrestle with the decision to sign or not to sign a bill that forbade discrimination on the grounds of sexual orientation, the "Gay Rights" bill. Some two years before that, a similar bill was before the Wisconsin State legislature, and many Catholics had posed the same questions Cuomo was struggling with.

Cuomo responded to his critics by saying that the heart of the question is where private morality ends and public policy begins. He asked: "Am I obliged to seek to legislate my particular morality; and if I fail, am I then required to surrender stewardship rather than risk hypocrisy?"[2] Cuomo says he sought his solution in the words of John F. Kennedy, who held that "the Constitution said that where matters of private morality are involved—actions that don't harm other people or deprive them of their rights—the state has no right to intervene."

TENTATIVE DISTINCTIONS

This scenario can help to show the complexity of the issues involved and the need to make some distinctions. Although it has been overused, there is a distinction to be made between private and public morality. One should not deny that distinction. In our discourse we assume, for example, that masturbation or the use of contraceptives is private morality. I am sure we would not want the state to intervene in such private matters. The question, however, remains: How does one distinguish between what is private and what is public? One could answer that public morality affects the public

46

order and the common good of the whole society, and thus needs regulation for the good of all.

But even this assertion can be modified by some exceptions. Another distinction that had been made historically by Catholic authors from Augustine to Thomas Aquinas centered around the lesser of two evils. It was presupposed that the state should not legislate on all moral issues. Augustine saw public prostitution as the lesser of two evils, and many Catholic countries have permitted it on the same grounds that Augustine did. He wrote: "What can be mentioned more sordid, more bereft of decency, or more full of turpitude than prostitutes, procurers, and the other pests of that sort? Remove prostitutes from human affairs, and you unsettle everything because of lusts."[3] Aquinas himself, in his wise treatise on human law, states that "the natural law is a participation in us of the eternal law; while human law falls short of the eternal law ... Wherefore, too, human law does not prohibit everything that is forbidden by the natural law."[4] In that same article he also states: "Wherefore human laws do not forbid all vices from which the virtuous abstain; and chiefly those that are to the hurt of others, without the prohibition of which human society could not be maintained."

In these authors we find two arguments brought forward: Not everything that is forbidden by natural law needs to be a part of human law, and sometimes the principle of double effect means that for a greater good, one does not try to legislate against all moral evil in a society.

But are homosexual relations a subject of private or public morality? If it were just a question of two consenting adults in private, one could say that it would be private morality, but homosexual relationships have ceased to be a question of private morality in our society. I would have to admit that there are many aspects of the gay subculture that I find contrary to the gospel and also harmful to public order; for example, the promiscuity related to gay bars and baths and the sadism of the leather bars.

Could a Catholic nevertheless hold to a position that laws which discriminate against homosexuals because of their sexual orientation alone, especially in the area of employment and housing, should be changed? I believe a Catholic could in conscience sustain that position. One does not seek to deprive couples living in concubinage of civil rights. One could defend such a position as not legislating in favor of homosexual unions but only in favor of their rights as citizens. This seems to me to be within the compromise positions held by Augustine and Thomas Aquinas. Wisdom tells us that not all morality must be incorporated into law.

A second scenario that was experienced in Wisconsin in the early 1980s dealt with bills that fall into the category of "consenting adult bills." Many of the old blue laws were still on the books of Wisconsin. For example, even fellatio in marriage was punishable by law. I am sure that the police had a glorious time trying to enforce that one! Adultery and fornication were also crimes. If the police had to arrest all the young (and not so young) couples on the east side of Milwaukee who were living together but unmarried, or if they had to arrest every person in the richer suburbs guilty of adultery, our jail system would have become larger than our stadium. These laws were either unenforceable or left themselves open to whimsical and selective enforcement by those in charge and, as such, were bad laws. They could be considered outside the realm of public order. Some argued that to change them would make it look as if society—including the churches—was condoning immoral behavior and that such laws have an educative value.

Unenforceable laws are bad laws, and a Catholic could well hold to that position even in the case of clear moral issues such as adultery and forni-cation. But it is true that many in our society, including Catholics, believe that everything that is not punishable by law is morally permitted. There is an educative value to good law in terms of instructing people. That this is the role of the state could be questioned. It is certainly the role of religion. It is up to religion to inculcate good morals into the lives of the people and to inform them that there is a distinction between what is legally permissible and what might be morally right.

Governor Cuomo raises another difficult question for the Catholic Church in the U.S.A.: How permissive can the society become in terms of legislation that touches morality in order to respect the pluralism of views out there? I believe we would all answer that the Church must feel free to participate in the public forum on all such issues in order to come to a consensus about them. Such a consensus will never be complete or totally to the Church's liking. For the Church not to be involved in the debate on moral issues, sexual or societal, would be to deny its very nature, but it can never expect that it will be able to persuade the entire population of its positions, and thus Catholics must live with such ambiguity.

It is often difficult for the Church leaders in their teaching positions to support such ambiguous and imperfect legislation, but I feel it must at times do so. In most instances this will be done through the positions taken by individual Catholics and less frequently by the positions the Church takes as a body. But Catholics must at all times keep in mind the distinctions mentioned, so that the faithful do not take what is a partial realization in law of the Church's morality as the whole of that teaching. Probably in most cases it is advisable for the Church leaders to remain neutral in the public forum and to leave freedom to the individual Catholic lay person in the political scene, depending on how each one views the repercussions of such imperfect legislation on the whole well-being of society.

It is helpful to note that it should not always be the role of the Church leader to solve all these questions but rather to point out the limits within which the Catholic lay person should act while experts sort out the results. Often I find myself asking only if one could, as a Catholic lay person in politics, hold a certain position and not whether it would be my position or what I might deem best. In that respect, I believe we must trust more our lay people when they feel they must compromise and cannot bring into legislation the fullness of a Catholic moral position. For most of these issues there is much debate on how one analyzes the data present.

Underneath all this discussion lay diverse ways of seeing how religion relates to public policy. Governor Cuomo stated that he received many vicious letters for not vetoing the gay-rights legislation. I can assure you that my mailbag was also full of such letters heaping abuse on me because I did not fight the repeal of the blue laws, unenforceable as they may have been. Underneath all those letters lay diverse ways of seeing how religion should relate to public policy. I would like to analyze the different presuppositions in the minds of those who wrote. Some of their positions can be found in almost every epoch of the history of the Catholic Church.

MODELS OF CHURCH-STATE RELATIONSHIPS

I would like to outline four models of how religion relates to public policy, their historical antecedents, and how they are still with us today.

Model I could be called the *privatization of religion*. This privatizing of religion is almost a presupposed part of American "civil religion." I divide this model into two varieties. The first, Model I-A, states that religion is a private affair between me and God. Robert Bellah wrote this, about our first model:

Religion is now relegated to the purely private sphere where it is to be considered merely one of a variety of possible private options. Accompanying the subjectivization or privatization of religion, already under way in the eighteenth century, is the tendency to depoliticize religion . . . religion was no longer seen as the bearer of a public truth. Religion along with all sorts of superstition and metaphysics could exist as fantasies in individual minds, but the public world was to know only instrumental reason in the service of human progress and this worldly perfection.[5]

Even very devout religious people often interpret the separation of Church and state in the U.S. political tradition in this way: The pulpit should stay far away from the political arena.

One finds a similar sentiment, but for different reasons, in the Far East and in Hindu and Buddhist cultures. There the aim of religion is to take one outside the narrowness of this world; one seldom sees any relationship between religious beliefs and social concerns. For example, in the many meetings which we Benedictines held between monks of the west and Buddhists, one had to be raising the point constantly that there was a relationship between religion and social concerns. Some religions tend to be modes of escaping from this world and of denying that this world has any value. For Catholics that question was clearly settled by Vatican Council II and the pastoral document on *The Church in the Modern World* (*Gaudium et spes*), where the values of this world are recognized for the true values that they are.[6]

There is a more subtle form of this first model which I find among lay people today, especially in the Catholic Church. I will call this Model I-B. These people quote Vatican II, quite correctly, as stating that the sanctification of the secular order is the special mission of the laity. This is done by the private work of each individual according to his or her status in life. But then they add to this vision a new form of "laicism"; they assert that the institutional Church should have no role in public policy but just in preaching the gospel and nurturing the faithful through the sacraments. The institutional Church is allowed to run schools, including colleges and universities, hospitals, nursing homes, and other charitable institutions, but is not permitted to engage in the political debates which affect such work, except through the private channels of the laity. Model I-B does not deny that political issues also have moral and ethical dimensions which are a part of the concerns of religion, but it contends that the only way in which the Church as institution or as a societal body can and should enter into the dialogue is through its individual members, not collectively. Many lay people do not say this position publicly but imply it often by their negative response to Church statements about social and political issues. Insofar as I understand the theology and ecclesiology that underlies the *Opus Dei* movement, I see elements of this model in their practical solution to how lay and clerical should relate with regard to issues that touch society and politics.

Model II could be called the *monastic model,* or that of flight or separation from the world. There have always been Christians who have left the normal relationships of society to form their own miniature world. Monks set up an alternative model to the Roman society, one that was taken over by the institutional Church in the post-Constantinian period. There has always existed the temptation on the part of some Christians to try to escape the tensions of living with others in a pluralistic world by forming their own ideal society. Recently I read an advertisement in a Catholic paper from a group of Catholics, a bit disillusioned with the Church and society today, who have bought property in Virginia and are now developing a town for orthodox Catholics only. In their schools they will see that only the true doctrine is taught; they are advertising for "old-fashioned" priests, especially retired ones, to join their town.

Cults, almost of their nature, tend to this kind of withdrawal, as the Jonestown experiment so sadly proved. There is a difference, however, between negative withdrawal from the world, such as we experienced in hippie communes, and genuine monastic flight. The former does not hope or expect to affect society or make it better by such withdrawal. The monastic intent has always been to give its charism back to the Church and world by showing a correct ordering of values and sustaining those engaged in bringing about value changes in society.

This withdrawal from the political order in order to preserve one's religious integrity was common at the time of any persecution and can easily be understood under such conditions. Our ancestors often came to America with similar motivations. More recently one saw the Church in North Vietnam do the same. After the Communist takeover in the late 1940s, Catholic families went into a kind of self-made ghetto in order not to have their children contaminated by Marxist doctrine. As a result, when the unification of the churches in North and South Vietnam came about some years ago, the Church in the north had remained as it was in 1948, never having heard of or been influenced by Vatican Council II. Temptations to do likewise in Eastern Europe were avoided; there the Church struggled openly and forcefully to retain its position in society. We all find Model II tempting at times, but it has never been a long-enduring model in the history of Christianity.

I would not want to end this description without referring to some Catholics who take a prophetic stance over and against the culture we live in. These heroic souls do so in order to make society better. Such a stance is well within the Catholic tradition, since it attempts to make society better through its positions. They do not retire to a ghetto but remain solidly within the society.

Model III could be called the religion-state or the *state-religion model.* Here the Church states that Catholicism must be recognized as the religion of the state and be accorded a special place and status in law. Other religious bodies are permitted to exist, but their public role and expression are severely restricted. Many of my vicious letter writers belonged in this category. Although they would not want to admit that they are intolerant of others' views, still, from what they write, one has the definite feeling that they espouse the position that truth has all rights and error has none. The assumption underneath this model is that ultimately the aim of the Church is to make the moral order of the Church correspond to that of the legal order and that the Church is the guardian of that public moral order. This position, in its extreme, was taught by the integralists of the last century, because they asserted that the Church's ideal or model of society should be completely or integrally realized in actuality in every society. This model was officially advocated within the Catholic Church after the Reformation and the religious wars that followed it. *Cujus regio, ejus religio.* The intimate bond between state and religion made it impossible to conceive of permitting another religion to enter into full rights, since in that case one feared persecution and ultimate extinction. This model came to the U.S.A. and was upheld by many colonies before the Declaration of Independence. Under the new pluralistic model that evolved later, Catholics at first felt uneasy, since Rome and their European counterparts saw acceptance of pluralism as a betrayal of the traditional Catholic position. In spite of years of struggling to show that this third model was never the model of the Catholic Church in the United States, one finds many traces of it among our people and others. I still find threats of it today in what is left of the Moral Majority. Ted Kennedy had every reason to say, in his address at Liberty Baptist College, founded by Jerry Falwell: "[Women and men of deep religious faith] may be tempted to misuse government in order to impose a value which they cannot persuade others to accept."[7] It also seems to me that the State of Israel is trying to belong to the twentieth century and yet is plagued by Orthodox pressures that wish to keep it in Model III. We see the same model in many Muslim states where religion and the state are connected. The Russian Orthodox Church is struggling with this model as it faces up to the new regimes of the old Soviet Union. Will it try to hold on to the outdated model that made it a department of the state? If so, it will hamper its own pastoral development and freedom.

Sometimes it seems to me that single-issue people, such as some members of the pro-life movement, fall into this category and work out of this model. Although I would hold quite strongly that abortion is a moral evil and that it does belong in the realm of public order and morality and is not just a private affair, I also know that we are far from forming a consensus in the public arena and must continue in the public debate to convince through the power of reason and truth itself. The Prohibition experience has shown us that laws without persuasion end in disaster.

We see remnants of this model in the thinking of some in the Catholic Church. There is perfect logic in the position Archbishop Marcel Lefebvre held, if one looks at the position he took against the *Declaration on Religious Freedom* in Vatican II. He remains known today in the U.S.A. mostly for his retention of the Mass in its so-called Tridentine form and in Latin. That is but symbolic of a deeper underlying ideology on his part. Profoundly influenced by the *Action Française* movement, he retained the state-religion model as the only one that could be a safeguard of faith. One sees this model operating in many conservative newspapers, such as *The Wanderer*, in their treatment of political issues and the Church. It was, for example, foreseeable that they would not accept the position of the American bishops some years ago in support of the Hatch amendment. That amendment would have given us a slice of bread when it was impossible to have the whole loaf. To the integrists, that is heresy. These positions linger on because they have not been touched by the newer insights of Vatican II.

THE NEW MODEL OF VATICAN COUNCIL II

I would like to proceed now to the model that emerges from Vatican Council II—Model IV. But first, I must say a word about concepts that led up to the change of position. (By the way, we should not be surprised that the insights and vision of this council have not yet penetrated the whole of the Catholic Church and its structures. The full vision of Vatican I did not come into being till almost a century later, in Pope Pius XII. The Catholic Church moves slowly!)

Two men in particular prepared the way for the model that came out of Vatican Council II: Jacques Maritain and most especially John Courtney Murray, S.J. Maritain's break with the *Action Française* and his polemics against them did much to prepare Europe for what was to follow. In our own country, the work of John Courtney Murray had a similar impact, but one that has not yet reached its full force.[8]

What Murray saw as new to the world scene and as forcing a rethinking of the state-religion model was the rise of constitutional government. What had been traditional in the United States became, after the Second World War, common to almost all European nations. Constitutional law permits society to put limits on the role of the state and its intervention. Murray thus distinguishes between society and government. Society is the larger category that comprises, in addition to government, the social, religious, cultural, and economic orders which ought not be subsumed by the state. Murray saw the common good as the aim of the whole of society and thus limited the role of the state to that of public order—that is, an order of justice (which safeguards the rights of individuals in society), an order of peace (which enables human beings to live in harmony in society), and an order of public morality (necessary for people to live together in society).

It was at the time that these distinctions were becoming clear in the writings of John Courtney Murray, S.J., that Vatican Council II took place. Two documents in that council were to corroborate his research: *The Church in the Modern World* and the *Declaration on Religious Liberty*. The effects of these two documents have not yet been totally felt in Catholic circles. After finishing the decree on the nature of the Church, *Lumen gentium*, the bishops were not totally satisfied with their work. It had been too abstract and did not answer the problems of the relationship of the Church to contemporary problems. Under the leadership of Cardinal Suenens of Brussels and Cardinal Montini of Milan, they began a second document to confront these questions. In section 40 of that document a new term is used to express the relationship between Church and World: interpenetration. I use it to name Model IV: the *model of interpenetration*. The traditional Augustinian terminology of the "two cities," when used in this document, find them not juxtaposed, but growing up together. For this reason the document treats freely of the contribution of the Church to society and of what it receives from society. It also discusses other aspects of society that the Church interrelates with: culture, economic life, and the political community.

Section 76 on the political community and the Church is especially important for our models. The first paragraph of that section makes a clear distinction between the activities of Catholics acting individually or collectively in their own name as citizens and activities done with their pastors in the name of the Church. Thus the council rejected as insufficient Model

I-A and I-B as I described them above. Next it rejected what I called Model III (state-church) in these words: "The Church, by means of her role and competence, is not identified with any political community nor bound by ties to any political system. It is at once the sign and the safeguard of the transcendental dimension of the human person." The paragraphs that follow in that section are a brilliant statement of the specific mission of the Church to preach the gospel and the need for political freedom to do so.

This leads me to the other document of Vatican Council II that is of importance for Church and politics: *Declaration on Religious Liberty (Dignitatis humanae)*. Chapter I of that document makes a statement with unparalleled consequences for Church-state relations and becomes the second basis of Model IV. It states:

> The Vatican Council declares that the human person has a right to religious freedom. Freedom of this kind means that all people should be immune from coercion on the part of individuals, social groups and every human power so that, within due limits, nobody is forced to act against their convictions in religious matters in private or in public, alone or in associations with others. The Council further declares that the right to religious freedom is based on the very dignity of the human person as known through the revealed word of God and by reason itself. This right of the human person to religious freedom must be given such recognition in the constitutional order of society as will make it a civil right.

Having assumed that position, the Fathers of the council were accepting as normative for the future a religious pluralism in society. One could not have it both ways: Accepting this freedom of conscience in religious observance does away with Model III and lays the ground for Model IV—interpenetration of Church and society, indeed a society that is religiously pluralistic and in which constitutional law limits the role and influence of the state. The role of the state remains that of the public order. The Church can nevermore ask for preferential treatment. On the other hand, this separation does not signify that there is an absolute separation between political and moral issues. It simply means that in the public debate to arrive at a public consensus, the role of the Church must remain that of being one of many in the dialogue, with no preferential status except the force and strength of the arguments produced or the wisdom from her tradition.[9]

After the issuing of the U.S. bishops' document entitled *Challenge of Peace: God's Promise and Our Response*, one of the television channels in Milwaukee did a series of programs on the Church and politics. One of their questions put to me was: Can a bishop command his people to vote for a certain law or for a certain candidate? The bishop could command anything he wishes, I guess, but in the light of the above, the conscience of each individual would have to decide how to vote. I know that fears still exist in the minds and hearts of many who are not of the Catholic faith that there will develop a strong Catholic voting bloc under the dictates of the bishops. Personally I feel sure that if I were to tell the Catholics of Milwaukee to vote for a certain candidate, they would most definitely vote for another. To my way of thinking, there is no Catholic voting bloc, not in the sense that Catholics vote according to some ideology. I believe Catholics vote—like most citizens—according to how they think it will affect their pocketbook and seldom from a single, clear religious motive that is shared by all.

PRACTICAL CONSEQUENCES

I would now like to draw some practical corollaries from the above discussion.

The Catholic Church will not align itself with a political party, but remain in the pluralistic freedom offered it. Historically Catholics were probably more inclined as immigrant groups to join the Democratic Party, while the bishops tended to be Republicans. Today that may have shifted some, but it seems to have no influence on how the Church relates to public issues. In fact, the Church today is quite unique in the positions it holds: It was more allied with the liberal Democrats on the nuclear issue and the capital punishment debate and allied with the conservative Republicans on the abortion issue. Pope Pius XI's position on subsidiarity and government would please the most right-wing Republican, but when Pope John XXIII talks in *Mater et magistra* about the need to balance this authority with a clear socialization, he sounds like a Democrat.

In the light of this nonalignment, the Church has forbidden—without special extenuating circumstances—priests and religious to run for office as a part of party politics. The concern is that the priest or religious in question would be seen as speaking for the Church, that the Church could become too tied into one party, or the individual could lose his or her freedom to preach the gospel and be limited to a party platform or to the wishes of a constituency which may not reflect the full gospel message. (I believe for sisters the question could be argued somewhat differently, since they are not clerics and thus do not canonically have the same status, although they are perceived in the minds of most faithful as representing the Church.)

My second corollary is this: *The Church seeks only the freedom to be a part of society and to be able to work toward the common good and public order through the normal political processes.* Thus the Church does not interpret separation of Church and state as a separation of the Church from society or as a separation of religious concerns from political issues.

This desire to be a part of the social fabric will require a new kind of discipline in a pluralistic society, if the Church is to be faithful to the norms she has set up for herself in the document on religious freedom. This social role will continue to engage the Church in educational and cultural activities at all levels, in health care and other charitable services, in social work for the poor and needy, and also in that most important task of forming the consciences of those who will listen on the vast range of sociopolitical issues that fit under the accepted title of justice and peace. She will be both active and persuading.

Finally, *The Church's role cannot be defined solely in terms of her political involvement.* The role of preaching the gospel and of sanctifying human persons, that is, of continuing the full mission of Christ on earth, has a transcendental dimension that one could not call political per se. Preaching the gospel will change the hearts of people and thus transform or change society, but the result can only be called indirectly political.

It is not always easy to find the line of distinction between private and public morality in concrete cases; it is not easy to see what is the common good in a complex situation; it is not easy to determine when the state must come into action to maintain the public order; but I can tell you that these distinctions found in the two documents of Vatican II have given me a framework within which I, as bishop and as a citizen of this country, have been able to bring my religious beliefs to bear on the public debate, respecting at the same time the pluralistic society in which we live.

New issues from the Milwaukee scene greet me each day as I read the newspaper: Is it permissible for the police to enter a home in a case of child abuse without a search warrant? In my mind I say yes, because one of the roles of government is to protect the rights of the voiceless; this is the order of justice. Is it proper that the Posse Comitatum stock up arms and form its own police system? No, only the state can use force; it alone has the duty and power to maintain the order of peace. There are a-thousand-and-one other issues where the judgment will be less clear, and I feel sure the public debate with all people of goodwill will help me to sort out what is the common good.

In this way, I would hope that the people of the Church of Milwaukee, my primary faith-sharing community, would fulfill the description of the Church given in the pastoral constitution *The Church in the Modern World*:

> With loyalty to the Gospel in the fulfillment of its mission in the world, the Church, whose duty it is to foster and elevate all that is true, all that is good, and all that is beautiful in the human community, consolidates peace among all peoples for the glory of God (#76).

CHAPTER 5

The Church in Worldly Affairs

Tensions between Laity and Clergy

The Church in the U.S.A. is passing through a new and critical phase with regard to two aspects of its life: How its clergy—and especially its bishops—will relate as teachers to its highly intelligent and trained laity, and how the Church as a whole will enter into the debate in American society on political, social, and economic issues.[1] These two questions are intimately related and involve a further analysis of what was said in the previous chapter. In both areas the experience in Europe has been different from our own and has led there to much bitterness and anticlericalism, especially in the last century. By examining some of that history and reflecting more deeply on what is unique in our own experience, we can avoid some of that negative fallout and create the atmosphere for a more optimistic future. This present moment is a crucial one for such an analysis because the bishops of the U.S.A., through their pastoral letters, especially those on war and peace and on economic justice, have raised these issues in a new and urgent way.[2]

What I write here are reflections on my experience as a member of the drafting committee of the Bishops' Conference preparing the pastoral letter on the economy. Underlying the process involved were many ecclesial questions that will demand a broader vision and should provoke a deeper response on our part as Church. The inevitable tensions that result in these two areas—the teaching authority of the bishops and the laity, on one hand, and the role of that same teaching authority in political, social, and economic issues, on the other—require a calmer and clearer analysis and a more profound and nuanced response for the future. A new functional model of Church is at stake.

CURRENT SITUATION: A FORMED LAITY

One of the greatest assets of the Church in the U.S.A. is its well-trained laity. No other group of Catholics in the world can boast of such a high degree of education. Undoubtedly this is the result of our school system on all levels and the emphasis that was put on education by the immigrant Church. Getting ahead in the U.S.A. meant education. Our Church insisted on this education for its people and sought to provide it. One can debate about the quality of the education provided in some sectors, but the thrust and drive were always present and have reaped their rewards, especially since World War II. At times we complained that the religious education of our laity did not keep pace with the level of their secular education, that our people were expected to take their places in society, business, and academia with only grade-school religious training. They still had only child-like concepts that did not and could not cope with the questions raised on the adult level. I am certain this has been true in many cases, but the fact remains that our well-trained laity represents the finest asset we have in the Church in the U.S.A. today and is the source of its strength and vitality. I think, too, we are only beginning to see the importance of that trained laity. The clergy and religious who brought them to that point can be justly proud, as all teachers should be when their pupils begin to move out on their own and break loose from any infantile dependency on the teacher.

Nevertheless, in all honesty, several negative factors must also be mentioned, since they affect the present moment. I want to reflect on some of them.

First of all, *pro dolor*, it must be stated again that Catholic social teaching has not been assimilated by our Catholic population. I have had occasion to reflect on this elsewhere, but it must be repeated to understand the current situation. Some of the causes mentioned may have stemmed from the abstract nature of these papal documents, their tendency to speak only out of a European experience, their hesitancy with regard to the American democratic experiment, the custom in religious education to keep to cate-chetical formulae that did not touch social and political issues, the American mentality of religion as a private affair, and so on. Whatever excuses one gives, it is evident that Americans of the present generation had to confront their new arrival into mainstream political and social life without the aid of a well-developed social doctrine at hand. This has resulted in a pluralism among Catholics in the U.S.A., healthy in some respects, but not derived from thought-out positions of how events and the decisions they require relate to the whole of Catholic tradition and teaching.

If such a lacuna is evident in this one field, one can assume it might also be present in others. One could ask, for example, if Catholic physicians and administrators of our health facilities have sufficient background in medical ethics. On a more pragmatic level, one sometimes sees the deficiency of a clear concept of what Church is all about in the dynamics of parish councils, finance committees, and diocesan pastoral councils. How the laity is to live its life as Church in the marketplace makes even more demands on its training. I do not feel we should blame the laity for these deficiencies— they are a part of the whole Church—but rather attribute this lack to the all-absorbing concern of our forbears, as a minority group in a predominantly Protestant culture, to keep the integrity of their faith. They did not foresee the need to prepare themselves for leadership in the larger societal structures.

Simultaneously there existed in the Church in the U.S.A. a tendency to assimilate the American political experience without critical judgment. The negative reactions of the Church in Europe to much of the philosophy of the Enlightenment, with its concepts of freedom from all restraint, of democratization tendencies even in religion, of the glorification of the individual to the detriment of the common good, and even the suppression of religious institutions, did not correspond to the American experience. In fact, curiously enough, the Church in the U.S.A. defended the political arrangement here as good for the Church and its growth, but at the same time criticized forcefully many of the materialistic and individualistic aspects of the economic situation, even though its capitalistic roots were found in the same Enlightenment philosophy. (Perhaps these differences between the Church in the U.S.A. and the Church in Europe have still not been worked out.)

Nevertheless, the American political experience has affected deeply the U.S. Catholic laity, especially its attitude on separation of Church and state. The laity, as mentioned earlier, regardless of the degree or sophistication of its education, has been touched by the interpretation of such a separation as meaning a separation of political, social, and economic issues from religious and moral implications. Religion is still to many a private and personal affair. People say that the clergy should speak about "spirituality," which for them means an inspirational faith that does not challenge them to social involvement. They do not deny the need for virtuous lives and expect religious authorities to speak about personal virtuous living but not to make the next step into concrete social action for justice. The new biblical thrust of spirituality in the U.S.A. is beginning to challenge that approach.

There are others who are not so naive as to think such a separation of the political and social from the religious and the moral is feasible or desirable, but they have a fear that if the Church speaks out on the morality of political and social issues it will divide its members or deprive individuals of some of the valid options for action open to them. Intelligent lay Catholics rightly do not want to look like clerical puppets. In other words, the Church in the U.S.A. has yet to find a way of addressing political and social issues in an enlightened manner that respects the knowledge, competency, and conscience of the individual Catholics who comprise it.

CURRENT SITUATION: THE CHURCH AND WORLDLY AFFAIRS

The agenda for the Church in the U.S.A. for the next decade must be based on the document of Vatican II, *The Church in the Modern World* (*Gaudium et spes*). A sign that that agenda has not been completed is the confusion in the minds of so many over the relationship between the gospel and worldly affairs. They ask about the meaning of papal statements which do not permit clergy and religious to be involved in politics but which, at the same time, speak out so forcefully and cogently against injustices of a political and social nature. How is the Church to carry out the political agenda of denouncing injustices without seeming to be involved in politics? Is the priest who makes statements from the pulpit similar to papal or curial pronouncements or practical applications of the same to a local condition becoming involved in politics in a way that is out of keeping with his role as a religious leader? These and similar questions were frequently posed to me at conferences in the years we were writing the pastoral letter *Economic Justice for All.*

Let me list again some of the ideas of Vatican Council II that require in-depth reflection today. The Church's end or ultimate purpose cannot be reduced to a political agenda; nevertheless, the gospel that the Church proclaims and preaches will affect society here and now, not just a future world. How is that gospel to be lived in political, social, and economic life? The Church has no social blueprint for the perfect society, but she does preach the practice of justice and love, virtues that should transform relationships in every society. What is a just society today? Science has its own autonomy; there is no Christian law of gravity or Christian addition table. But the way human beings make use of these objective laws within society does imply the seeking of definite goals and aims and thus poses moral issues, not purely political or economic ones. The role of the laity is to transform secular society from within. It is to bring the gospel message to that society. In doing so it is truly Church. But does the laity act alone or with others, with Church members, with believers, with nonbelievers? If so, how? How does the faith community support them in their endeavor?

It seems evident that a new moment is upon us when we must reflect on the best aspects of our American tradition and on the way the Church should relate to the world. The problem is just as important for the Catholic laity as for the clergy: It is a question of how the Church should function within our pluralistic democratic structures and be truly a leaven and a sacrament to the world.

PRE-VATICAN II EUROPEAN MODELS

Vatican Council I (1869–1870) took place at a moment of crisis for the Church in its relationship to the new political structures of those times. The new governments, in addition to depriving the Church of its material and political power, tended to deny it even its right to existence. The first schema on the Church prepared for that council had three paragraphs and several canons on Church-state relationships. These were never voted on or even publicly discussed by the bishops because of the abrupt ending to the council, but since they were published as a part of the agenda, they were hotly debated in political circles at the time. The intransigents defended the old position of Pope Boniface VIII of the two swords, the Church being supreme over the state with the right to pass judgment on the latter's acts. The more realistic developed a new theory called *thesis* and *hypothesis*. Thesis postulated the ideal situation, in which the Church would be recognized as the state religion and where the laws of the state would reflect Church moral teaching. Hypothesis recognized that at times, by force of circumstances, the Church would have to live under other kinds of regimes, where it was to demand at least the liberty necessary for its own development. This second position was only tolerated, however.

This unfinished agenda continued to be debated into the period of modernism at the end of the century, when the more rigid view became labeled integralism. Those Catholics who sought a complete or integral Catholicism in the political realm demanded the perfect coalescence of Christian morality with the legal realm of the state and thus the suppression of all error. No concept of separation of Church and state was considered orthodox. Wrong has no rights, they said; and, since the Catholic Church was considered the source of all truth, its doctrine alone should dominate in political affairs. This position was slowly eroded by political developments but continued to exist in some textbooks until World War II. It certainly affected Church-state attitudes in some areas of Europe and especially in Central and South America.

Although this position was not sustained by Vatican Council II's document on religious liberty, it still colors much Catholic thought in our time. Today, when one reads some of the literature from the more aggressive Catholics who become rather fixed on winning on a single issue, one wishes that there would be more clarity with regard to legality, morality, and compromise. Moreover, when one hears Fundamentalist preachers talk on political issues, one senses that traces of integralism are still much a part of the whole American religious scene. Many non-Catholics still fear that if American Catholics ever obtain a majority in political power in the U.S.A., they will per force put into effect, by edict of their bishops, the integralist positions of the last century and deny the rights of other positions to exist. The fear of the "Catholic threat" has not died.

Integralism will always be a temptation for the Catholic Church—or for any group convinced of the rightness of its positions. It can only be checked by the attitudes prevalent in *The Declaration on Religious Liberty* of Vatican Council II, attitudes that see the use of force—psychological or physical—as immoral, as an abuse against conscience, and call out instead for persuasion by rational arguments as the only way to obtain political consensus in the public forum. The Church has a valid role to play in such a building of consensus as an equal partner with all others in a pluralistic society. But our heritage of integralism will still be a temptation because of its clarity and simplicity.

In the immediate period after World War II, since the thesis-hypothesis position was no longer practical, a new model became more prevalent in Europe, although its germs go back to prewar discussion and reflection. As more and more European nations abandoned monarchies and as Fascism and Nazism were suppressed by force, new and more democratic models of government arose. The Church had to react to these models and find a way of taking its role in society—a society where it had once held a dominant position. One could call this new model of Church that arose a kind of *Catholic Action model.* It prevails in Europe today.

In this new model the role of the clergy, especially the bishops, is one of teaching. That teaching remains on a theoretical level and does not descend to concrete situations and cases. These are left to the laity, whose task it is to put the theory into practice. This process of putting theory into practice can take place in two ways: the first is by individual action on the part of Catholics in the world (the *Opus Dei model*), the second and more visible way is by Catholic movements. Thus there evolved in Europe Catholic political parties, Catholic labor unions, organizations of Catholic industrialists, and so on. These groups are the lay arm or branch of the Church. When one group seems to lose its impetus and drive and becomes sterile, a new one comes forth (for example, note the rise and rapid success of the movement Comunione e Liberazione in the last decades in Italy). As one can see, these movements are based on an ecclesial model and not just on pragmatic principles. They see a clear distinction between clergy and laity that corresponds to a teaching authority and its implementing force; they call this subsidiarity, using the word in a kind of expanded sense. Do these new arrangements solve the tensions between clergy and laity? Should this model be adopted for the Church in the U.S.A.?

First, let me list some of the advantages of this functional model of Church. It does get things done. It can accomplish much because of the clear structure for political and social activity it offers the lay Catholic. It keeps the teaching model of the Church in a traditional framework and postulates a clear identity for the clergy as they relate to political and social affairs. In so many respects it is attractive because the bishops and priests keep their hands clean and do not get involved in the messy turmoil that political and social issues can bring with them.

The negative aspects are also numerous, however. Even though the impression of lay independence is given on the surface, it is generally assumed (at least by many in countries like Italy) that the clergy are still secretly pulling the strings. The laity can appear to be the puppets of the clergy, especially of the bishops. In concrete terms, for example, many still ask how strong the Vatican influence is on the Christian Democratic Party in Italy.

Moreover, it does not solve the question of a legitimate pluralism of action on the part of the laity in implementing theory, for the positions of the lay movements can become very dogmatic. Leaders of these movements often question the orthodoxy of lay persons who operate by choice outside such approved structures or have other political persuasions. In other words, they do not face up to the following decisive question: Is there only one lay arm of the Church, or can there be many? This model in practice seems to deny alternatives.

History also shows a tendency among the lay models to return to the position of integralism. This accusation is frequently made, for example, against the group Comunione e Liberazione in Italy. A zeal to christianize the world can soon lead members to equate in their own minds their movement and its aims with the divine plan for the Kingdom. That the Holy Spirit may be operating outside such organized movements through other forces in society is seldom considered. In addition to dividing the laity itself, these movements can also tend to divide the bishops. Their members often consider those bishops to be orthodox and thus to be listened to, who agree with their own stance. Others who do not support their positions are labeled disloyal. The neat division between laity and clergy soon falls apart in practice, and new tensions between clergy and laity arise.

One last important aspect of the relationship between Church and world is left unsolved by this model. Among the many practical concrete options open politically and socially at a given moment of history, one should not assume that the choice of the morally most acceptable solution is an easy one and self-evident, even if the theory is clear. In other words, the debate cannot cease at the transition point from theory to praxis. Such a neat, deductive kind of moral process is idealistic and does not correspond to life's experiences. New circumstances can call into question aspects of existing theory. The "teachers," to understand what is going on, must be a part of the whole process, otherwise their positions will always be taken too late to be helpful. Hidden within this model is not only an ecclesial concept but also one of methodology for moral decision making, a methodology that is foreign to the American inductive cultural and educational processes. The Church in this model, moreover, often loses credibility, since it is rendered too slow in condemning concrete cases of injustice (Nazism in Germany or Fascism in Italy).

For all these reasons Catholics in the U.S.A. would be wise to take a critical stance toward this European phenomenon of lay Church movements and accept the fact that they do not correspond to our historical experience and do not solve some of the crucial questions we are asking at this moment of history. These movements were hotly debated at the Synod on the Laity in Rome in 1987, and many of the pitfalls were pointed out there.

THE MODEL EMERGING IN THE U.S.A.: CLERGY AND LAITY COOPERATION

It is not possible at this moment for the Church in the U.S.A. to delineate an alternative that would be as clear and neat as the European model. Some of its characteristics, however, can be outlined, but with some hesitancy, because its full development has not taken place.

It is becoming more and more evident that, in the process of reflecting on the political, social, and economic issues that our society faces today, it is important to keep a unity of clergy and laity. The present process for writing pastoral letters has been more effective because of the consultation process involved. Through that process the bishops have been able to hear from all proponents of different points of view within the society. In all of these recent documents, there comes a point when someone must decide what is and is not consonant with Catholic teaching. In the case of the Economic Pastoral Letter, the bishops exercised this role conscientiously. One thing, however, was clear: The concern for orthodoxy or truth was shared by all. The search for orthodoxy is not a clerical prerogative. The Church has every reason to be concerned about the integrity of its doctrine as well as the consistency of its tradition. Ultimately this responsibility must lie with the teaching authority, but not separate from reliance on the knowledge and expertise of lay and clergy alike.

Although the consultative process has functioned well, one might ask if there still could be another process, more ongoing and less cumbersome, that would permit both clergy and laity to be active and involved in reflection on contemporary issues that face the Church and its involvement in specific issues of our society. Perhaps the dialogue should be predominately among the laity, with the role of the bishops being that of asking crucial questions of the protagonists, of clarifying the tradition, and of creating the structures needed for fairness and comprehensiveness. Perhaps the most important contribution of the clergy should be to keep clear the pastoral implications of the dialogue so that the whole Church can profit from them but not be prematurely led into action when the religious and theoretical basis is not yet clearly articulated.

Two major reasons suggest themselves for thinking out a new process. First of all, the subject matter is so complex and difficult today that no group of teachers could be expected to master all the diversity and intricacy of the material. It is difficult to imagine any group—bishops certainly included—who would have, on one hand, a developed knowledge of recent biblical exegesis, systematic theology, and moral systems and, on the other, a refined knowledge of politics, business (on a world scale), nuclear armaments, medical procedures, genetic engineering—to name just a few of the areas where moral decisions must be made today. The second reason is that bishops should not be placed in a position of always reacting *post factum* to decisions made by others. This has been true in the past with less damage done because of the nature of scientific experimentation. Now the possibilities seem relatively limitless and the decisions on which possibilities should be pursued are the urgent ones. Post factum will be too late and constantly places the whole Church in a reactive position, not in a leadership role.

Perhaps we should think out new processes which will permit bishops to function credibly as teachers in these complicated moral issues that range from MX missiles to leveraged buy-outs to decisions based on genetic analysis. For them to be effective teachers, they cannot be separated from the debate, nor can they be constantly writing long and comprehensive documents that would remain more and more in the realm of pure theory. We need a more nuanced concept of a teaching Church and a teaching authority that corresponds to the complex reality of the current situation. Perhaps just short statements of encouragement and caution are all that is needed as bishops, priests, and laity struggle over these complicated issues. I am convinced our laity are intelligent enough to differentiate when the bishops want to speak with the full force of their moral authority—whether it be on a moral theory or on its practical application—and when they are still as undecided as everyone else and are in the process of weighing conflicting values and trying to sort out the right direction. I am sure bishops would be relieved to know that they do not have to have all the answers all the time. In this way the delicate question of the degree of specificity with which bishops should speak could be seen as a false one, since the Church lives in a very specific world—bishops as well as laity—where theory and application are in a living dialogical process.

THE EMERGING MODEL IN THE U.S.A.: THE CHURCH IN THE WORLD

Since the presidency of John F. Kennedy, the Catholic Church has found itself in a new position in American society. In all areas—political, social, economic, and intellectual—it has assumed a significantly new role. Nevertheless, the new situation has brought with it new tensions. One does not solve these tensions simply by saying that individual Catholics, wherever they may be in society, must act according to their consciences, since that begs the question. How does the Catholic tradition form their consciences and, when the laity act, how does it relate to the whole Church as a community of believers who hold to certain beliefs, values, and practices? One cannot talk about all those issues in the abstract, and so it is necessary to try to reduce the problem to the issue that becomes the touchstone of them all—compromise.

For this reason it would help to reflect on one aspect that is true of the political sphere but also of the whole of life, whether it be economic or social, namely the principle of compromise. In a real world the ideal is never fully obtainable. *The Pastoral Constitution on the Church in the Modern World* (*Gaudium et spes*) and the *Decree on the Laity* recognize that imperfect nature of the world but never say exactly to what degree the ideal must be realized. In other words, they never touch on compromise.

The most difficult question posed to the Church today by the American political process is precisely that of compromise, a solution inevitable in a pluralistic society. The whole theory of integralism returns to haunt us at this point of the discussion. Vatican II rejected integralism, but it did not delineate where compromise must stop. I do not at all believe the European division between clergy and laity solves this question. It does not "save" the Church from compromising its positions by letting the laity do so. The laity is Church as fully as clergy. The laity does not have a different kind of conscience from the clergy that permits more compromise on its part in a pluralistic society.

When does the Church say no compromise is permitted or that the ultimate degree of compromise has been reached and one can go no further? Thomas More was not the first, and will not be the last, to raise this question for his personal conscience. It surfaces again and again in the abortion debate when one asks what is expected of a Catholic politician. Are there issues where the Church will not compromise in trying to bring its moral perspective into the political and social order? The laity asks: Would the authorities please name these? (Abortion under all circumstances?) Are there issues where the Church will compromise? (Divorce laws?) Would the authorities please name these? If the authorities say "no compromise" and demand this of all the faithful, what happens when a majority of Catholics are not convinced of the no-compromise position? (Birth control under all circumstances?) If the Church is unsuccessful in obtaining by rational argumentation a consensus on her position regarding an issue facing society, what does she demand of her members, who must live in that society and hold office there?

To me these are the real issues we face as Church today in the U.S.A. They will not be solved by splitting us into a lay branch for the concrete and a clergy branch for the theory. They are not solved either by placing the solution on the conscience of the individual Catholic lay person, who is kind of thrown out into the world without support. Ultimately the question must be resolved in the conscience of each one, but the role of the supporting Church should be to help form conscience.

Given the state of the debate on these issues, I would suggest the following guideline: That we do not fall into a new integralism in politics or in business, but that we accept the sincerity of those who differ with our point of view, as we work toward a consensus. This means we enter into the public debate to persuade others and arrive at a consensus. If that consensus is not in our favor, we should not demand "no compromise" on the part of all Catholics involved in the political arena or in the legal realm. If we did so, we would exclude all Catholics from politics and society and render ourselves again a ghetto. In the economic field, we should not assume that everyone who disagrees with our solution is immoral, but rather continue to challenge each other as to the moral values inherent in each solution proposed, the compromises that must be accepted, and the effectiveness of varying solutions. For example, those who espouse minimal government must be forced to face up to the question of who will provide the social services needed, and how. Those who advocate government solutions must show how errors of the past are to be avoided, how welfarism in its pejorative dependency mode is to be avoided, and the like. Sustainers of both positions can be considered as searching adherents to the gospel message.

Grappling with compromise, as distinct from an integralist position, is the unfinished agenda of the pastoral constitution on *The Church in the Modern World*. I would suggest we move very carefully in declaring any position to be one without compromise (unless the individual conscience so declares it) as we work toward a consensus on any issue and before we have obtained consensus in the wider political arena. In this way we can respect fully the American social and political processes, we can respect in politics and business the integrity of our competent lay and clerical members, and we can move the debate further by reasoned arguments.

More than anything else, we need at this moment in the U.S.A. the time and freedom to evolve that functional model of Church in political, social, and economic issues that corresponds to our tradition. Cardinal Gibbons fought so strongly to avoid Catholic separation in social and political issues in his fight to avoid "Catholic" unions. We would do well to keep his wisdom in mind today. The functional model of Church that would result would not be so neat and simple, but it would correspond more clearly to the complicated world we live in today.

CHAPTER 6

Principles for the Relation
of Church and Government

I write as a bishop, not a politician.[1] Bishops have the advantage of not having to run for office at periodic intervals (though some probably wish they did) and should speak of human and social issues out of a different context.

In his farewell address, George Washington said: "Of all the dispositions and habits which lead to political prosperity, religion and morality are indispensable supports. In vain would that man claim the tribute of patriotism, who should labor to subvert these great pillars of human happiness, these firmest props of the duties of men and citizens." Since religion and politics are both flourishing in our U.S. society today, it would be worthwhile to reflect on how they should relate to each other in this democratic, pluralistic society that is ours. That is the theme of this article.

RELIGION AND THE TEMPORAL ORDER

Religion is indeed strong in America and has entered the political debate in the last decade in newer and more visible ways. We have witnessed the new political aggressiveness of the Fundamentalist religious bodies, and for the first time in the history of our nation, the Roman Catholic Church has been caught up publicly in debates on many political and social concerns. For these reasons it is good and wise that we begin to dialogue on our respective roles and clarify the scope and limits of our interventions. I would like to proceed, first, with a series of interrelated propositions that enunciate how I believe religion relates to the temporal order, and then draw some conclusions that might be helpful for future discussion.

1. We all must adhere to the wise insight of the founders of our nation on the clear separation between Church and state: No religion should ever be declared our state religion, and no religion should enjoy preferential treatment before the law. All churches have a right to participate in the

social and political debate, to be an active part of the social fabric of the nation, but without privilege.

But we also hold that this separation of Church and state does not mean that political and social issues are without moral and religious content. We feel that many of the political issues our nation faces do have moral and ethical dimensions. For this reason religious bodies feel they must enter into the debate. Some issues may indeed have little moral content: administrative details, choices of contractors, or whatever. Others may be fundamentally moral in nature, although never exclusively so: civil rights, nuclear war, abortion, capital punishment, pornography. Most lie somewhere in the middle. Rarely are there choices between absolute good and absolute evil, but most often between one good and another good where the trade-offs have to be carefully weighed.

In so many of these cases, the political and religious dimensions are a question of overlapping rugs in the same household. Politics, by its nature, must be the art of the possible. With limited resources and with so many points of view and interests to be reconciled, politicians must often find ways of satisfying all concerned and balance many conflicting currents. Religious leaders can be more prophetic, more demanding, less compromising, less flexible. Their duty to society is to keep the moral principles clear in the midst of the concrete imperfect realization of a moral ideal.

Spiritual leaders, like the prophets of old, tend to seem negative for that reason. As irritating as their voices might seem, their moral point of view is often very needed, even if the morally perfect cannot be here and now fully realized. Their intervention should not be taken as negative carping. I guess I am asking the pragmatic politicians to be patient with the more prophetic, idealistic religious leaders, since the latter, too, serve society by keeping its moral perspectives high.

2. No religion should become a political party or align itself with only one political party. I can say clearly and without hesitation that the Catholic Church in our country will not align itself with any particular party. Such an alignment would be bad for politics, but worse for religion.

Thus it should not surprise you if the Catholic Church seems to be politically ambivalent, aligning itself nationally with the conservative and right wing of the Republican party on issues such as abortion and with the more liberal Democrats on many social issues, capital punishment, and the rights of labor. At times this can be confusing, and I always smile when people assume that, since a religious leader accepts one aspect of a party platform, he or she accepts a whole series of issues connected with that platform. (For this same reason it is often difficult to nail down where a religious leader is coming from, since it is not from within a party system or platform but from a whole other series of considerations and traditions.)

Again, what I would like to emphasize here is that no church should align itself with a political party, since churches have a different scope: Proclaiming a gospel message that may or may not be consonant with a party platform but which must remain independent to be true to its prophetic self. It is for this reason, too, that the Catholic Church does not permit priests, under normal circumstances, to run for public office. A priest's mission of preaching the gospel could become compromised by the need to represent a constituency or to be loyal to certain party policies that may be religiously ambiguous.

At the same time, religious bodies do ask for the freedom to be themselves and to take part fully in the life of society without being discriminated against by legislation that would seem to exclude them.

3. There are two ways in which a church enters the political debate: through the opinions and actions of individual members of that church, and through statements or pronouncements that come from the official bodies of a religious group. It is in this area where we as religious bodies must clarify whom the speaker represents and the weight behind the voice. We, for example, consider each Catholic, by reason of baptism, truly missioned by the Church in his or her secular vocation.

I want to quote from the "Pastoral Message" that accompanies the pastoral letter, *Economic Justice for All*, on this point:

> The pursuit of economic justice takes believers into the economic arena, testing the policies of government by the principles of our teaching. We ask you to become more informed and active citizens, using your voices and votes to speak for the voiceless, to defend the poor and vulnerable, and to advance the common good. We are called to shape a constituency of conscience, measuring every policy by how it touches the least, the lost and the left out among us. This letter calls us to conversion and common action, to new forms of stewardship, service and citizenship.[2]

But we certainly would not want all Catholics to feel that the positions they take or the opinions they voice must be the official positions or opinions of their Church. Yet we know that some issues will be much more central to their Church's teaching and thus less open to compromise and debate. We wrestle with the need of the politician to be true to that faith commitment and yet free to work out the pragmatic solutions that are realistic in any given situation. We do not have absolute clarity on those points yet.

At times the officials of a church, acting in their teaching capacity, will sense a need to enter the debate, either on a national or local level. We bishops have done so more recently with the pastoral letter on nuclear deterrence and again on the economy. We do so regularly through organizations such as the United States Catholic Conference of Bishops' Office in Washington, D.C., or through state conferences and other ecumenical organizations. Here, too, churches tend to be selective, often picking issues of direct concern to their well-being: school issues—public or private; issues of larger societal implication where the Church feels that moral dimensions dominate—for example, pornography, abortion, living wills. In this latter category it is often difficult to determine the degree of specificity with which a church should speak out, as its role is not to draft specific legislation. Sometimes, however, one cannot talk about a moral issue without being very specific; this is especially true about medical ethics. Here, too, we as churches have to clarify how we enter the debate on such societal issues of a moral and ethical nature, so that our moral authority does not get lost in contingent details that change rapidly. I am sure we will continue to learn by experience in these areas and become more explicit on how to differentiate between individual and corporate voices.

4. The areas of chief concern for the Roman Catholic Church today that do indeed overlap with political concern are those that touch human life and society. The bishops of the world, at the Second Vatican Council in Rome in 1965, laid out three areas where the Church would hope to contribute to the whole of society: 1) safeguarding human dignity, 2) strengthening the seams of human society, and 3) imbuing everyday human activity with a deeper meaning and importance.[3]

Safeguarding human dignity is the reason that for a hundred years now the Church has been involved in the rights of the working person and has developed a strong tradition of moral values concerning the workplace. The Church's concern about family and what may weaken family structures is characteristic of the second category of those elements that strengthen the seams of human society. Giving meaning to life should overarch all the Church's interest in education and human development. In sum, one could say that the issues most important to the Catholic religion today deal with the human person: the dignity, well-being, and social integration of that person.

5. Finally, the Church's role cannot be defined solely in terms of her temporal involvement. The role of preaching the gospel and of sanctifying human persons, that is, of continuing the mission of Christ on earth, has a transcendental dimension that one could not call per se political. Preaching the gospel will change the hearts of people, make them more virtuous and honest, and thus transform or change society, but the result can only be called indirectly political.

COROLLARIES FOR REFLECTION

From these propositions that enunciate how I believe religion relates to the temporal order, I would like now to draw three conclusions.

1. The Catholic Church is still struggling with how it should relate to constitutional governments. Its history in this area outside the U.S.A. has been mostly a post-World War II phenomenon—a period relatively short in the long history of the Roman Catholic Church. Here in the United States the Catholic Church has enjoyed great freedom, but only after the

period of John F. Kennedy has it begun to enter more fully into the national debate on social and political issues. Before that it spoke mostly to its own constituency on very specific political issues where Catholics had a direct involvement. Since the U.S. experiment of the separation of Church and state was seen by most European nations as good, it was imitated for the most part in the formation of the Christian Democratic parties around the world, with a certain amount of struggle. These debates coalesced into a statement of the bishops of the Second Vatican Council on religious liberty:

> The Vatican Council declares that the human person has a right to religious freedom. Freedom of this kind means that all people should be immune from coercion on the part of individuals, social groups and every human power so that, within due limits, nobody is forced to act against their convictions in religious matters in private or in public, alone or in association with others.[4]

Having assumed this position (put forward by the American bishops and vigorously sustained in debate by Albert Cardinal Meyer, former Archbishop of Milwaukee), the Roman Catholic bishops of the world accepted as normative for the future a religious pluralism in society. One could not have it both ways. That was 1965. We struggle with how that is to take place so as to avoid religious indifferentism, on the one hand, and uncompromising rigor, on the other. We can never ask that all law under such a constitutional government mirror Catholic morality; but we do see that law also has its own didactic force in the morality of a society. We know that under such a constitutional arrangement we must do more to alert our people that not everything permitted by law is morally acceptable to Catholic standards. We have been negligent in this regard. The Church must also be concerned about private morality, while the role of the state is more restricted to public order and thus public morality. We have yet to learn how all of this should work out to allow the politician the freedom that must be there and to keep religion a vital social force for good, not just a private affair.

My first conclusion is that we as Church are still struggling with this recurring theme of political compromise on moral issues.

2. It seems to me that George Washington was indeed correct and that religion and government have more interests in common than one would at first surmise. Government, too, must be concerned about justice for all and the common good of all.

Earlier I mentioned the Church's concern for human life and human dignity. In Catholic teaching, human rights include not only political and civil rights but also economic rights. Pope John XXIII stated that all people have a right to life, food, clothing, shelter, rest, medical care, education, and employment. Striving to fulfill these rights is the duty of the whole of society, of which government is indeed a part. The "Pastoral Message" states:

> This does not mean that government has the primary or exclusive role, but it does have a positive moral responsibility in safeguarding human rights and ensuring that the minimum conditions of human dignity are met for all. In a democracy, government is a means by which we can act together to protect what is important to us and to promote our common values.[5]

Our tradition makes a distinction between charity and justice, and the Church must be concerned about both. Charity must indeed increase, yes, even radical charity. But it is not the answer to all of society's ills. It does not create jobs or necessarily help people develop their skills for the job market. We see justice in its biblical roots as a broader concept, one that permits everyone to participate in sharing the goods of society. Here churches must talk about both greed and laziness in the same breath. For these reasons churches will be interested in unemployment, welfare, and all those areas that affect human dignity and help or hinder participation in society.

It is a religious belief that all people are equally sacred to God. This leads to a special concern for those who are not making it in a society. It leads to a special concern for the poor and any whose human dignity has been harmed. It should not be strange if the Church feels it must be that voice of the poor and continue to call out for those who are marginalized in our society. We are asking that we all work to integrate all others into society. If this is not a priority of our nation, we will be forced to continue to call out. We have not found the answer to minimizing the human costs of a dynamic capitalist economy. The displacement of people, the retooling of their skills, and the resulting fears of insecurity are real costs that affect the human person deeply. They must be religion's concern for that reason; but they are also, and one could say primarily, government's business, for elected government is the instrument of our common concerns.

A dynamic economy is, of course, the way to put people back to work and the only ultimate remedy for the poor. But in the meantime we cannot slacken our concerns and our efforts and must work together toward humane solutions.

I am convinced, too, that religion should be of greater help in eliminating some of those evils of our society that militate against incentives to work, and in this way the Church contributes to the whole of society. Here religion should become a more active voice against those breakdowns of morality and customs that affect the whole of society, such as sexual promiscuity, bearing children out of wedlock, divorce, and the like — all of which affect the stability of the family, the primary cell of any sound society.

My second conclusion is that religion and government have many common goals in this area of creating a more stable society.

3. Third and last, the tradition of Catholic social teaching has always been positive toward government, seeing it as having a necessary, positive, if limited, role. The role of the politician is seen as a calling, a noble vocation of service to others. Earlier I cited a document of the bishops of the world on the relationship between religion and the temporal order. That same document from 1965, after encouraging civic and political formation for all, but especially for youth, states: "Those who are suited ... should prepare themselves for the difficult, but at the same time, the very noble art of politics."

It is good to repeat those words, *the noble art of politics.* We have too easily today forgotten that politics, rightly understood and practiced, is indeed a noble art. We have lost such positive words as *statesman* and *diplomat* to express this noble art. I salute all of those who take up that vocation.

I would hope that they would strive to avoid the temptation of letting that art be debased by a lack of civility and decency, such as scandalized some in the last electoral campaigns and which only lowered esteem of the vital, positive role of the politician in society.

If I were to sum up the major theme of this chapter, it would be that alluded to in Washington's farewell address: politics and religion, both being concerned about the human person in society, have so much in common. When both function properly, they reinforce each other and both contribute to a just and peaceful society where the individual person can flourish and develop. Catholic social teaching accepts the threefold division of society into the state, the private economic sector, and what are often called "mediating structures." Religious groups belong to those mediating structures. A society functions best when the state, the private economic sector, and such mediating structures as churches can agree on a basic vision of society, one that supports the rights of the individual but also reinforces the ethical duties and obligations that accompany such rights. Working to foster the common good of all then becomes the task of each one of us, working within our own specific area of competency.

PART III

FAITH AND MONEY

INTRODUCTION

One of the difficulties endemic to Catholic social teaching, since it is derived mostly from papal documents, is that it is always very general in tone, fitting the varied situations of Catholics living throughout the world. Pope Paul VI saw this problem and, in a true spirit of subsidiarity, asked each nation to undertake its own analysis in its own nation in the light of the tradition. In his apostolic letter entitled *Octogesima adveniens* (1971)[1] he points out this dilemma and encourages the various countries to pursue the task of local analysis:

In the face of such widely varying situations it is difficult for us to utter a unified message and to put forward a solution which has universal validity. Such is not our ambition, nor is it our mission. It is up to the Christian communities to analyze with objectivity the situation which is proper to their own country, to shed on it the light of the gospel's unalterable words and to draw principles of reflection, norms of judgment and directives for action from the social teaching of the church. . . . It is up to these Christian communities, with the help of the Holy Spirit, in communion with the bishops who hold responsibility and in dialogue with other Christian brethren and all people of good will, to discern the options and commitments which are called for in order to bring about the social, political, and economic changes seen in many cases to be urgently needed.[2]

The American bishops in 1980 took that admonition seriously and tackled the whole question of capitalism and the U.S. economy in the light of Catholic social teaching. The process followed that recommended by Pope Paul VI and, with its extensive consultations over many years all around the nation and with all its ecumenical and interfaith partners, perhaps could be considered just as important as the contents. The work continued for over five years and involved the publication of three public drafts of the document. This process was also based on the successful one used for the Peace Pastoral. The final draft of the Economic Pastoral, *Economic Justice for All: Catholic Social Teaching and the U.S. Economy*, was presented to the bishops in their fall meeting in 1986 and overwhelmingly approved by them.

Although the bishops through the decades had commented on economic issues, especially when a particular need arose, the only previous attempt of this magnitude went back to 1919 to the document *Program of Social Reconstruction.*

The first mandate given to the drafting committee in 1980 was to try to approach capitalism theoretically, as had been done in a previous pastoral letter on Communism. This attempt was dropped when it seemed that the document that would result would be an academic treatise and not a pastoral letter. When it was also discovered what a lengthy and gargantuan task it would be to analyze all the many theories of capitalism and free market economy—from Galbraith to Friedman—in the U.S. and around the world today, the drafting bishops felt they had to limit their work to that which was possible. For this reason they decided to treat the actuality of the system now functioning in the U.S.A. and how its results related to the social tradition of the Church. In addition, it sought to see how the system affects, positively and negatively, the rest of the world, especially the third world.

In many ways, I regret that there is so little systemic analysis of capitalism in the document that resulted. Most of the criticism from the political left points out this weakness. Third-world theologians in particular found this lack disturbing. They also pointed out that there was no consistent sociological and political analysis, that is, no articulated political philosophy, behind the document. Many of these criticisms are valid and were a necessary consequence of the original decision to limit the work. As a result, for example, there is no clear analysis in the document of the relationship between power and wealth. That weakness is apparent and needs further updating.[3]

Although there was a hope that the international section would be fuller, it did not come forth as a centerpiece of the whole document. If the document were to be done over today, I feel sure it would include more on the global nature of the economy and also about its ecological repercussions. No one can today discuss the economy of the U.S.A. in isolation from the economic theories and practices of Japan and Europe. For example, there is almost nothing about banking, in spite of its importance in the international scene. Could one perhaps persuade the Swiss bishops to reflect on that aspect of Catholic social teaching!

The first task of the committee was to ferret out of Catholic social teaching and that tradition those principles that would be important in analyzing the U.S. economy. The best formulation of the thinking of the committee in that regard can be found in the "Pastoral Message" that accompanied the full document. It is a summation of the principal themes of the Pastoral Letter itself. In that message the bishops outline six points that act as a kind of overall umbrella for the analysis of the ethical characteristics of an economy. I would like to reflect on those points as an introduction to the contents of the letter itself. They sum up its major concerns.

First of all, the bishops state: *Every economic decision and institution must be judged in the light of whether it protects or undermines the dignity of the human person.* Unfortunately, it seemed necessary to reiterate that an economic system has to help people. It is people who count, and the system must serve them, not vice versa. The bishops state in the letter that one must judge a system by what it does for people, what it does to people, and how it permits people to participate in it. This basic orientation has been reiterated many times by Pope John Paul II. The bishops made it their own and used it as the beginning of their analysis. It is easy also to show a philosophical basis in natural law, as well as a scriptural basis for that proposition.

The second proposition was this: *Human dignity can be realized and protected only in community.* This proposition caused some problems to many who had not been accustomed to thinking in terms of common good and had not seen that the obligation to love one's neighbor had a dimension that goes beyond just an individual commitment. Later in the letter the bishops develop that theme at great length and even project a kind of new American experiment that involved all levels of society in the decision-making process that affects their economic life. I would have to be honest and say that this section, although it is biblically sound and Aristotelian in basis, frightened many who have been much affected by the hyper-individualism of the U.S. climate and culture. For this reason, the bishops were called socialists by many conservative economic thinkers. I have noticed, however, that throughout the nation, because of this proposition, many universities (Catholic as well as non-Catholic) have held seminars on the question of common good and what that concept means in a U.S. context.

The third basic principle of the American bishops is: *All people have a right to participate in the economic life of a society.* This statement simply means that basic justice demands that people be assured of a minimum level of participation in the economy. It is in this paragraph where the bishops talk of economic rights and show how the need for shelter, food, clothing, and so forth must be fulfilled if people are to become participants in society. The whole question of employment also becomes essential in this discussion, and one could rightly say, as some have, that the bishops' letter turns out to be a cry for an ethic of participation on the part of all. This is a far cry from the criticism on the part of some that the letter is a welfare letter. Just the contrary: The letter demands participation through work.

The fourth principle is the following: *All members of society have a special obligation to the poor and vulnerable*. In analyzing this principle, the bishops cite so many convincing passages from the Old and New Testament. It is true that some have felt the philosophical basis for this idea came from the theories of John Rawls, but there are some basic differences between the bishops' approach and that of Professor Rawls.[4]

The bishops' approach finds its source in the concept of justice and rights and the need to support the common good of the whole by assisting those who are not able to participate. One could say that because there is more need on the part of the poor, there is also more obligation on the part of others to be of assistance. Later in the document this principle is also spelled out in terms of international relationships between wealthy and poorer nations. It seems that the American people were not ready yet to follow through on that principle, but it stays there as one of the greatest challenges of the letter itself. The term that was used, of course, is the "option for the poor," even though that has received an ambiguous interpretation on the part of many.

The next principle is: *Human rights are the minimum condition for life in community*. This principle comes, of course, from the writings of Pope John XXIII. It is the whole of society, the bishops stated, that must protect these rights and it is not just the duty of the private industrial sector.

The final principle is: *Society as a whole, acting through public and private institutions, has the moral responsibility to enhance human dignity and protect human rights*. When one talks of rights, one has to talk in the same breath of responsibility and obligations. Both the safeguarding of the rights and the obligations that ensue fall on the whole of society, both the public and the private sector, not just on government. As mentioned earlier, this mix of private and public has been the subject of much debate. Those who espouse a totally free market with no government intervention, even if this never has and never will exist, feel strongly that this principle as enunciated by the bishops goes too far to the left. The bishops do not say that the government has a primary or exclusive role, but the letter does say that when the private sector or the free market is not functioning to protect the good of all, then it is the duty of government to intervene. That statement is in line with the best of Catholic social tradition, and there are many statements from that tradition to back it up. The bishops say that this is especially true in a democracy, where such a government is and should be under the control of the people and acting for the common good of all. I believe we will regret that this concern for the safeguards of the poor has been passing more recently to the corporate world. They are not under the control of an electorate through a free voting process. They are only vaguely responsible to the society, with no structures of accountability, and naturally inclined to use as a criterion for helping with societal problems their own self-interest. Their work for social justice, sometimes very admirable in itself, is seldom coordinated and usually no more efficiently done than it was previously by the government.

Although churches will naturally want to look at the way in which an economic system affects the lives of people, it is also legitimate for churches to look at the way in which people live out the gospel commands in any given economic system. For this reason, the American bishops have added a section at the end of their document on the responsibilities of the individual for a constant personal conversion, so as to acquire the attitudes that a follower of Christ should have toward material goods and the stewardship thereof. These issues are not easy to work out in practice, because each Christian has a different vocation in life and different responsibilities. Nevertheless, the document tries to lay out Christian attitudes toward this world and also what perils are in store for a Christian living and working in a system such as that found in the United States. It is a ringing call to conversion, to charity, and to justice, but, more than anything else, to love for all God's people in our nation and in the world. The gospel is not just a challenge to the American Catholic to think differently but also to act in a different way. The gospel demands new vision and selfless action. It is an attempt to break down racial and cultural barriers and see how people should and must relate one to another for the sake of the common good. It is also a way of breaking down the barrier between private morality "at home," if you will, and the morality needed today in the marketplace.

Finally, the Economic Pastoral Letter of the American Bishops of 1986 is also a plea to the Church itself to act as a just economic component in society. The Church is an economic actor and must abide by the same norms of justice as laid down for all entities in society. There is much work to be done in that regard, and we know that we are only at the beginning. Not only the pastors but the new lay leadership must also be convinced of the need for the Church to be a just employer. The next decade will not be an easy one for the Catholic Church as it attempts to unravel this issue for itself with honesty and courage.

In gathering together a few essays that were written in the last decade on economic issues and the Church, I have tried to select several that cover diverse questions, biblical as well as moral, to capture some of the ongoing discussion on these important topics. It is impossible to avoid overlapping, as often the same principles have to be enunciated in a different fashion for a diversified audience. That the letter itself occasioned so much debate and discussion is in itself a gain, as it forced people to consider economic issues from a moral point of view and not just from one of financial profit.

CHAPTER 7

God and Mammon

Money and the Kingdom

Because we Catholics have become a biblical people after Vatican Council II, we seek to find a vision for our way of life in the words of Holy Scripture.[1] We do not seek, like the Fundamentalists, to interpret every phrase literally, but we expect that our own contemporary attitudes of how God relates to us and how we relate to God will be consistent with that biblical vision. We also want our relationships among ourselves to correspond to the way Christ told us to relate to one another. For this reason, we read and examine the scriptures to attune our minds and actions to that biblical vision. Today it is not easy to do so, because we have come to the realization that everyone is our neighbor. We no longer can be narrow in our vision and limit our neighbor to those who share our own nationality.

CATHOLICISM AND GLOBAL ISSUES

At a symposium at Marquette University in 1985, an economist chided the Catholics who had spoken because they gave the impression that they were somehow obsessed with concern for all the poverty and misery in the world. "You Catholics," he teased, "seem to feel guilty about all that poverty out there in the world. It is not your fault. Don't be so guilty about it. Enjoy the wealth you have. It is God's gift."

Because we are members of a Church that professes to be catholic, that is, universal, we do see that we are in a peculiar way bonded with all people on this globe; we know we share their anxieties and their lot. I would suggest that the problem is not that we feel guilty about the poverty all over the world—often we do not feel responsible enough—but that we feel helpless and inadequate when we see so many of our brothers and sisters suffering want, starvation, malnutrition, and even death. The size of the problem can lead to a certain paralysis: We feel it is beyond us and exceeds the means

80

directly at our disposal or within our power. We then hide behind anonymity. What all are responsible for, no one is responsible for. We Catholics have nothing to be ashamed of if we are concerned about the poor; in fact, as I hope to show, it is built into our very discipleship and following of Christ. We only have to be ashamed if we take no steps to find answers, if we permit ourselves to be frightened by the magnitude of the question, if we turn our backs on the poor and forget them as we go about our own mediocre lives, if we are scared off by those with jealously guarded positions of power.

Because the question is global, it also places on us Americans a special obligation at this moment of history: We are indeed the most powerful economic actor on the world stage. It is true that we are not the only actor and perhaps are perceived by others as more powerful than we are or than we perceive ourselves to be. The reality of our position is that we are indeed a key actor, the most influential; thus the attitudes and values we bring to the world scene will, for the most part, prevail.

It was good Pope John XXIII who first realized that the nations of this world have become economically interdependent and that this trend will not be reversed. He clearly outlined the moral obligations that result from economic relationships between richer and poorer nations in *Mater et Magistra* in 1961:

> The solidarity which binds all peoples and makes them members of the same family imposes upon political communities enjoying abundance of material goods not to remain indifferent to those political communities whose citizens suffer from poverty, misery, and hunger, and who lack even the elementary rights of the human person. This is the more so since, given the growing interdependence among the peoples of the earth, it is not possible to preserve lasting peace, if glaring economic and social inequality among them persists.[2]

At the end of that encyclical Pope John talks in greater detail of the cultural results of such interdependency and the need for reciprocal trust and an understanding of the demands of justice. In paragraph 59 he asserts boldly: "We affirm strongly that the Christian social doctrine is an integral part of the Christian conception of life."

A few years later, in *Pacem in terris*, he lamented that there was no political authority capable of maintaining the universal common good of the entire human family at this global moment of our history. He calls for renewed effort of each person on this planet to establish such right relationships based on love and justice. One could affirm that attitudes must change if structures of justice are to come about based on values and not expediency. The fact that we are seriously discussing such values in our day is at least a beginning to change. The purpose of the pastoral letter on Catholic social teaching and the U.S. economy was to continue our search for those gospel values that should underlie our society and its economic vision, as well. This article will examine some of the basic tenets of that gospel that should be our own today.

OUR BIBLICAL HERITAGE

The three concepts that emerge from our study of the biblical roots that affect our economic thinking on a local or global level are: creation, community, and covenant. The Creation story as related to us in Genesis shows that God created this planet and saw it was good. It is the work of his hands, thus no dimension of it is outside his care and concern. At the summit of creation stands the human person, made to God's image and likeness—male and female. They are given dominion over creation and thus stand as partners before God. The dignity of the human person comes with human existence itself and is prior to any division into races or nations or sex and does not depend on human achievements or titles or honors. The dignity and worth before God of every person on this globe is at the root of all Catholic social teaching; no one is excluded. The powerful are not preferred; the powerless are not in second place. The rich are not God's chosen ones; the poor are not those God neglects. For us Americans today, that truth is most important. The starving Ethiopian, the African pygmy, the Russian general are all equally loved by God and the object of God's care and concern. Christ, we learn, died for all, not for some privileged few. From this concept of the unique dignity of each person on the globe flow certain consequences that we call human rights. Pope John XXIII enumerated them for us—both the political as well as the economic rights. Among the latter he enumerated food, clothing, shelter, rest, medical care, and the like. Being born rich does not grant such rights, and being born poor does not deprive one of them.

Next we examine the concept of community. God's covenant is with a people. God is not only concerned about right relationships between us and God, but also right—or just—relationships that form a community. This birth of a people from the bondage of Egypt is the basis of Christ's preaching about a new covenant that would include all nations. If we want to merit the title *catholic,* we must have this kind of global or universal sense. The phrase "the human family" captures it best. The stormy period of the first century of the Church shows that this unity or bonding of all peoples was not acquired without stretching the attitudes of all beyond their limited national or racial origins. So it is in our day.

We bishops assert in the Economic Pastoral Letter that human dignity is not given to one by the community, but it is fulfilled and realized in community or in solidarity with others. New covenant solidarity excludes no one: "There is neither Jew nor Greek, there is neither slave nor free, there is neither male nor female; for you are all one in Christ Jesus" (Gal. 3:28). When we talk about the right to work or insist that full employment be a priority of this nation and indeed of the world, it is because we do not see how one can live out that personal dignity without access to participation in the life of society in solidarity with others. We are not calling for a welfare state; on the contrary, we are calling for a participatory society where some will not be relegated by the accidents of birth to paternalistic economic dependency or be marginalized economically because only a portion of the society will be permitted to work.

Our biblical roots in the covenant of Sinai also bring out another aspect of the society that marks our ethical vision. A special concern must be shown for the vulnerable members of the community: the widows, the orphans, and the aliens in the land. They lack political status and power, and so the covenant rules of society show a preferential option for those so deprived. Exodus 22:22–24 makes clear God's special protection for these powerless ones: "If ever you wrong [any widow or orphan] and they cry out to me, I will surely hear their cry. My wrath will flare up, and I will kill you with the sword; then your own wives will be widows, and your children orphans." The prophets do not permit the people to forget these demands of the covenant, especially if they exploit the orphans, widows, and poor. Note Jeremiah's strong statement to the people of his own day — a statement made in God's name:

> They grow powerful and rich, fat and sleek. They go their wicked way; justice they do not defend by advancing the claim of the fatherless or judging the cause of the poor. Shall I not punish these things? says the Lord; on a nation such as this shall I not take vengeance? A shocking, horrible thing has happened in the land: the prophets prophesy falsely, and the priests teach as they wish; yet my people will have it so; what will you do when the end comes? (Jer. 5:27–31).

These are the biblical roots of our much-used phrase "preferential option for the poor." Pope John Paul II defined that term this way: "a call to have a special openness with the small and the weak, those that suffer and weep, those that are humiliated and left on the margin of society, so as to help them win their dignity as human persons and children of God."[3]

To understand this concept, two lines of biblical investigation are needed: One is the difference between charity and justice; the other is the whole teaching in the Bible on wealth and poverty, on riches and the Kingdom. I would like to touch now on these two areas so critical to our understanding of our own Christian values today.

CHARITY AND JUSTICE

To most of us, justice has never acquired its full biblical meaning. Justice for us means that the punishment fits the crime or that the guilty get punished and the innocent are set free. Justice is blindfolded because it does not respect persons. Justice in the Bible is a much broader concept. It involves right relationships between the community or the person and God and among the members of the community as established in the covenant. The care of the powerless in the community is a matter of justice in the covenant—not one of charity—just as the right relationship to brother, sister, spouse are matters of justice. The poor are permitted in the levitical code to take food from others' fields, because that was justice. We have tried to resurrect this usage by calling such acts social justice, but they have not been too clearly defined as yet. We sense that they are based on the equality that comes from the human dignity of each person, an equality of opportunity that would rule out any handicap because of race or other external factor.

Charity, too, we have reduced from its broad biblical concept of love of God and neighbor to a kind of voluntary generosity. Our American concept of charity implies that we must be free to decide if we want to give, when we want to give, and how much we want to give. Seldom are we asked or expected to give from our substance. In the years we worked on the Economic Pastoral Letter, I received many letters from people who saw the poor only as objects of charity—voluntary charity—and thus protested against forcing taxpayers to pay for the poor. That something in the system might prevent the poor from getting work and taking care of themselves does not enter the discussion. Just treatment is not the same as giving leftovers. Biblical justice is not based on one's tax-deductible contributions, but on the needs of others that have to be met. Previous economists made a distinction, helpful in this case, between needs and wants. Needs corresponded to the economic rights spoken of earlier.

I will admit that charity, as we understand it, makes us feel good, while justice often frightens us and asks uncomfortable questions about the values of our society and where we really place the dignity of the person—of each person on this globe.

Charity in the biblical sense moves us beyond these categories to the story of the Good Samaritan and its implications. Charity includes justice and is bigger than justice, because it involves love based on God's point of view of the worth of each person.

I do not want to extend this thought but simply assert that concepts such as distributive and social justice, derived as they are from the fuller biblical vision, have not yet become a part of our Catholic concept of society today, and charity has not yet assumed among us the meaning Paul gave it in 1 Corinthians 13, where it is indeed the highest expression of our relationship to God and to others.

WEALTH AND POVERTY

When one comes to deal with wealth or riches in the Bible and the question of poverty, one is at first inclined to think that almost any position one holds can be supported by a biblical quote if one searches long enough. We have all seen articles published in some religious journals that quote passages from scripture showing that riches are a sign of God's blessing and poverty a sign of retribution or punishment. Yes, such texts do exist in the Bible and, thus, the need for a more careful analysis of these texts and these concepts. Unlike creation, community, and covenant, one finds a different treatment of the concepts of wealth and money in the discourses of Jesus than one might cite in the history of the Old Testament. This treatment by Jesus is very special in the New Testament. It is derived from the announcement that the Kingdom of God is at hand.

A certain ambiguity on riches does exist in the Old Testament, related to the idea that reward for just conduct will take place in this life. A threefold attitude is discernible. First, wealth is accepted as a blessing and a sign of divine benevolence. The promised land we see in Deuteronomy 8 would be full of springs and fountains, wheat and barley, vines and fig trees and pomegranates, of olives and honey. By fulfilling the covenant, these blessings will continue; neglecting the covenant will bring destruction. Proverbs puts it bluntly: "When the just man eats, his hunger is appeased; but the belly of the wicked suffers want" (13:25).

But this simple version of blessing and punishment did not correspond to experience and reality. Thus we find the constant question being asked: Why do the good seem to suffer and the wicked prosper? Job is unable to resolve that question satisfactorily.

We see the prophets, therefore, taking on a more realistic approach when they are more critical of the wealthy for their exploitation of the socially weaker classes. Isaiah cries out against such exploitation: "Woe to those who enact unjust statutes and who write oppressive decrees, depriving the needy of judgment and robbing my people's poor of their rights, making widows their plunder and orphans their prey!" (10:1–2).

Proverbs is full of such ambiguity, where the poor man is pictured as wiser than the rich. "The rich man is wise in his own eyes, but a poor man who is intelligent sees through him" (Prov. 28:11). This third attitude begins to see riches as closer to godlessness and poverty as true piety. Thus, Psalm 147:6 says: "The Lord sustains the lowly; the wicked he casts to the ground." Or in Psalm 37: "Be not vexed at the successful path of the one who does malicious deeds . . . For the evildoers still be cut off, but those who wait for the Lord shall possess the land . . . But the meek shall possess the land, they shall delight in abounding peace . . . Better is the scanty store of the just than the great wealth of the wicked. For the power of the wicked shall be broken, but the Lord supports the just."

Jesus, on the other hand, shows no such ambiguity about wealth and riches, because he does not teach a kind of reward or retribution limited to this life. The perspective that Jesus assumes toward wealth is clear: Everything is measured against the Kingdom he is announcing. First of all, the rich are not able to buy entrance into the Kingdom. Earthly possessions have no power to give the kind of new life Christ brings; it is and remains totally gratuitous. Increased wealth is not an assurance of entrance into the Kingdom, as we see in the story of the man who builds more and more barns and dies suddenly. Such a concept would be crass materialism of the worst kind.

In fact, the bias Jesus shows is against wealth as a facilitator of entrance into the Kingdom. "It is easier for a camel to pass through a needle's eye than for a rich man to enter the Kingdom of God" (Matt. 19:24). Wealth can so easily become an idol, depriving one of freedom of action and that kind of interior independence needed for choosing the Kingdom. "No one can serve two masters. You will either hate one and love the other, or be attentive to one and despise the other. You cannot give yourself to God and money" (Matt. 6:24). It is clear also that riches can color one's vision of reality and cause one to be inured to poverty and the sufferings that come from it. Note the Lazarus story, where the rich man is guilty by neglect; he failed to assist Lazarus at his door. Later, in his torments, he asks Abraham to send Lazarus to him to moisten his lips with water (Lk. 16:19–31). Riches still force him to see others as his servants, not as equals. Here riches keep the rich man from a true relationship with the poor. Such a right relationship is expressed by Luke in 14:12–14: "Whenever you give a lunch or dinner, do not invite your friends or brothers or relatives or wealthy neighbors. They might invite you in return and thus repay you. No, when you have a reception, invite beggars and the crippled, the lame and the blind. You should be pleased that they cannot repay you, for you will be repaid in the resurrection of the just."

The sole criterion that seems valid for the use of money and wealth according to Jesus' perspective is how it fits into the announcing of the Kingdom and his mission. He accepts the support of the women of Galilee (Lk. 8:1–3). He accepts the banquet at Bethany and the ointment in preparation for his burial (Mk. 14:3–9). Nicodemus and Joseph of Arimathea, wealthy Jews, are associated with him; he does not reject them because of wealth. He also does not reject Zachaeus, a minor tax official, who shares generously with the needy. Earthly goods are not rejected as evil—just seen as dangerous. Nor does Jesus ever say that the poor are ipso facto virtuous: that would imply they did not need the Kingdom.

Lastly, it is clear that the nearness of the Kingdom and the urgency to be totally free to announce it may demand of disciples an ever deeper renunciation of material goods. The disciples, when sent out on mission, must travel light. The rich young man, if he wishes to live in the company of Jesus as one of his intimate disciples, must leave all and follow him (see Mk. 6:7–12, Matt. 10:5–15, and Lk. 9:1–5).

I find it difficult to prove from the attitude toward riches in the New Testament that Jesus saw earthly riches as a kind of commodity entrusted by God to the stewardship of men, namely, that riches are to be multiplied so one can be a co-creator with God. The sole criterion of the use of riches is how they are to relate to the Kingdom, a Kingdom that is characterized as being preached to the poor, and to bring them the good news that brings sight to the blind, freedom to captives, and so on. Matthew 25 lists these works of the Kingdom, but such sharing must be demanded of all—not just the rich.

THE POOR AND THE KINGDOM

Who were the poor to whom the gospel is preached? Did Jesus show a preferential option for them?

First, we must be on our guard; we must not read the gospel according to our middle-class American mentality. At the time of Christ one could not really speak of a middle class. Indeed, *poor, middle,* and *upper* can be very relative terms, depending on our points of comparison. By the standards of Christ's day, most of us would fit into the wealthy class.

A distinction must be made between the truly destitute at the time of Christ and the more generally poor. Those who were desperately poor were often called wretched and pitiable. They were often the beggars, reduced to that state through being blind, lame, sick, ulcerated, and leprous—or having some skin ailment confused with leprosy. The custom of maiming children and reducing them to the status of beggar was not unknown in those times. The number of such destitute in Christ's time was larger than we in our culture might imagine. They often had no clothes and went naked or covered themselves against the cold as best they could. Some were mentally deranged—"possessed." Lacking basic necessities, they could not work and had to rely on the generosity of the less poor. Jesus performed many of his miracles for this class. In doing so, he gave proof that the Isaiah texts about the Messiah and the signs of the Kingdom were being fulfilled. The parable of the banquet shows that these beggars were indeed welcome into the Kingdom, as we see in Luke 14:12–13; one was to go to the highways and byways and bring in precisely this class.

Jesus himself was a carpenter's son and not a member of such a destitute class. Belonging to a carpenter's family, he would have been among the working-class poor. All his apostles were of the same class. Fishing was not a big business, and we frequently find the catch bad.

These groups stood over in opposition to the wealthy: the owners of the large landholdings parceled out under Herod the Great, those involved in tax collecting and other forms of trade with the Roman invaders, and those who were by profession attached to the Temple and made their living from service there. Jesus, in general, is harsh and uncompromising with that whole crowd. His many parables about daily workers for the large landholders would have resonated well among his hearers.

One could say that Jesus, being of the poor class, nevertheless identifies with the destitute by the form of his death. By the attribution of the Songs of the Suffering Servant of Isaiah to himself, he applies words characterizing the destitute to himself. In the fourth Song (Is. 52:13–53:12) he becomes one of the afflicted, compared to a leper.

The *Magnificat* has a similar reversal role, in that Mary is identified with the lowly and the powerless.

In both of these examples the important point is that God does reverse roles by sustaining the lowly and poor. Jesus thus can call the poor blessed; it is the meek who will inherit the land, and so forth.

The Sermon on the Mount is a remarkable moment in world history. The audience is the wretched and the poor. Jesus assures them that they are worth more than the sparrows or the lilies of the field, that they are precious in the eyes of his Father, that they should not worry about having no food or clothes because of their worth to God. These texts, spoken in that milieu, are certainly revolutionary. They gave to the wretched and poor a sense of worth and dignity not expressed in any other ancient culture. More than anything else, such words and such identification on the part of Christ give hope to the poor and a purpose in life. They acquire new expectations, since the reign of God, as promised by Isaiah and quoted by Jesus, is theirs. Rightly have authors stated that a movement for the poor could only have originated out of such a Judaic tradition, since its preparation was clearly introduced in the covenant and its importance was constantly emphasized by the prophets. Jesus built on that tradition and made it his own. The power class in Jesus' day understood that this teaching was not about rebellion against the Romans, but a class reversal within Judaism.

A preferential option for the poor does not mean that only the poor will be saved, or that all poor are virtuous, or that Jesus' prime concern was a sociological or class revolution. By asserting so strongly the value and worth of each one of those poor in the eyes of God, he did, however, lay the grounds for a rethinking of what it means to belong to a new universal Kingdom where all are equally welcome.

CONCLUSION

The question we must ask ourselves today, then, is how this biblical vision challenges us. If we live in a global world, then our neighbor becomes everyone in this human family. Our relationship to the poor on this planet, in particular, challenges the very basis of our faith. If Jesus Christ of his free will became one of them as an example to us, if he spoke of them as especially blessed, if he recalls their worth—the dignity of each one—then we cannot say the poor of the world have no hold on us as disciples of Christ. Somehow we know that our relationship to Jesus Christ and our membership in the Kingdom are tied into our relationship to the poor. These relationships cannot be separated. The poor of the world challenge us as they did the world of Jesus' time. Concern for them is integral to the credibility of the announcement of the Kingdom.

When the bishops' drafting committee began its reflections on the U.S.

economy, it was not their intention of doing a paper on poverty. In fact, the concern was that they might neglect the middle class. That the press picked up from the very first draft of the letter that it was a cry for the poor should be seen as a moment of grace and a blessing for all followers of Christ and those interested in creating a more equitable and just society. It has forced us to deepen our reflections on the poor and the Kingdom and undoubtedly will lead to a renewed examination within the Church by all of us of what discipleship or following Christ means in this moment of history and what our attitude must be toward the riches we possess in such abundance.

We will rise to the challenge to the extent that we permit the biblical vision — Christ's vision — to become our own. In prophetic fashion, I predict, however, that this vision will challenge us deeply. May we be open to the message!

CHAPTER 8

Toward a Moral Evaluation
of the Economy

Remarks before the Joint Economic Committee, U.S. Congress, June 16, 1986

An important part of public debate over economic policy is the set of values and assumptions that lie behind the technical debate.[1] As a religious leader, therefore, I want to focus attention in my remarks on the ethical content of economic decision making. I will do so in light of the draft pastoral letter on "Catholic Social Teaching and the U. S. Economy," a document that is currently under discussion and that will be voted on by all the Catholic bishops in November, 1986.

In pursuing a very public and extensive discussion of the draft pastoral letter, we bishops are attempting not only to educate Catholics about the Church's social teaching but also to stimulate a public discourse about the ethical dimensions of economic life. We seek to be a catalyst to join the moral and the technical, so as to overcome what is sometimes an excessive fragmentation of the various disciplines in society. We undertake this exercise with the firm conviction that a conscious effort to engage morality with economics will enhance the quality of moral discussion in our society.

Our Catholic tradition recognizes the value of technical competency and empirical accuracy in issues of public policy. These are clear prerequisites for the achievement of just and effective decision making in an arena as complex as our nation's economy. But these are not enough. Moral judgment based on sound values is also an essential element, for behind the maze of statistics and the rise and fall of economic indicators lie human lives and individual tragedies and successes. Behind the charts are real neighborhoods and cities and families deeply affected by the social consequences of economic decision making. It is precisely because these economic decisions ultimately affect human persons that economic issues must

90

also be seen as moral issues—issues that cannot be adequately resolved without considering the human and moral values that are inherently part of them. Therefore, the formulation and implementation of economic policies cannot be left solely to technicians, special interest groups, and market forces. They must also involve a discussion of the ethical values and the moral priorities of our nation.

We begin our pastoral letter by saying that any perspective on economic life that is human, moral, and Christian must be shaped by three questions: What does the economy do *for* people? What does it do *to* people? How can people *participate* in the economy? The basis for all of the moral norms presented in the letter is the belief in the dignity—the sacredness—of the human person. In short, the Church is interested in economic issues because the Church is interested in people.

At first, this concept of human dignity may seem vague, but it has many practical applications. Almost all the battles we faced in the U.S.A. to gain civil rights for blacks were battles for human dignity; all the struggles for decent labor conditions that were carried on at the time of the Industrial Revolution were struggles for human dignity; assisting workers affected by plant closings is a question of human dignity; standing with farmers as they see their life's work and heritage disappear is a question of human dignity. With that as background, let me comment on just four themes that are among those which are addressed in the pastoral letter: the social nature of the human person; the option for the poor; the protection of human rights; and interdependence on the global scale.

SOCIAL NATURE OF THE PERSON

Our teaching says that the person is not only sacred, but is also social. This truth today must be reinforced—particularly in our culture and our time, when individualism is frequently taken to extremes. Our tradition recognizes the value of individuality, but it also insists that we all are radically social. We require a social context in which to grow and develop fully. Therefore, the way we organize our society economically, politically, legally, and socially has a direct impact on human persons and their dignity.

Many would argue that we in the Church should focus all of our attention on personal and family values and avoid the social issues. They would like us, for example, to do all in our power to preach sound personal and family values to the poor, but not to address the broad social and economic issues that are involved in the issues of poverty. This very limited approach is inadequate in our view, for we believe that values are important at all levels—personal, familial, and social. The search for economic justice must be based on a respect for human dignity at all of these levels, since they are intimately intertwined.

Our concern for the social nature of the person leads us to put a strong emphasis on the themes of community and solidarity and on the need for all people to participate fully in decisions that affect their lives. The ultimate injustice is for a person or group to be treated as a nonmember of the moral community that is the human race. This is what we describe as "marginalization"—having no voice and no choice in the social, economic, and political structures of the society. The poverty of individuals, families, and communities is evil, therefore, not only because people's material needs are not being adequately met, but also because they are prevented from fully participating in society as active and productive members. They are cut off from the mainstream of American life.

In this regard our pastoral letter offers a strong challenge, stating that basic justice demands the establishment of minimum levels of participation for all persons. Where people are unable to find work even after searching for many months or where they are thrown out of work by decisions they are powerless to influence, they are effectively marginalized. They are implicitly told by the community: "We don't need your talent, we don't need your initiative, we don't need *you.*" If society acquiesces in this situation when remedial steps could be taken, injustice is being done.

Because work is so important to human dignity and to full participation in society, we say in our letter that full employment is the foundation of a just economy. The most urgent priority for domestic economic policy is the creation of new jobs with adequate pay and decent working conditions. We must make it possible as a nation for everyone who is seeking a job to find employment. In our judgment, the nation is not doing all that it could to achieve that goal. Therefore, we call for a combination of policy initiatives that would bring the unemployment rate significantly below the 6 to 7 percent range. These initiatives include broad fiscal and monetary policies as well as more targeted programs in both the private and the public sectors.

OPTION FOR THE POOR

In looking at the world, the Catholic tradition is concerned about the whole society. But we say the scriptures have taught us to have a *weighted* concern for the poor. It is not an either-or proposition, but we must give special attention to the poor. This theme, commonly referred to as the "option for the poor," is a basic and consistent one throughout Catholic social teaching. The biblical concept of justice suggests strongly that the justice of a community is measured by how it treats the powerless in society. As pastors, we bishops have seen firsthand the extent of poverty in our land. We have seen the long lines at our soup kitchens and our shelters. We have seen the effects of persistent high unemployment, of the massive shortage of low-income housing and the millions of families who are without adequate health care.

Above all, we have seen the damage poverty has done to children, the age group hardest hit by poverty in our land. If you are a child under the age of six in our nation, your chances of being poor are one in four. And if you are black, your chances are fifty-fifty. Seeing the economy in this way must surely motivate us to fashion a new commitment to eradicate poverty in America. For the children's sake and for our welfare as a society, we simply must do more.

Our draft letter suggests some elements of a national response to poverty—jobs and training for the poor, the promotion of self-help efforts among the poor, a reform of our educational system, substantial reforms in the welfare programs, etc. We don't claim to have all the answers and the technical solutions, but we do insist on the moral imperative to do more to alleviate poverty. It seems clear to us that economic growth in itself will not solve the poverty problem. We need more direct initiatives in both the private and the public sectors in order to deal adequately with this issue.

This theme of option for the poor suggests that part of economics is not only how we produce, but how we share. Thus the theme of distributive justice is a major thread running through the pastoral on the economy. We point to the high degree of inequality in our land in terms of the distribution of wealth and income and to the fact that the gap between the rich and the poor is growing. This trend must be reversed if we are to deal adequately with poverty and promote a real sense of community in the nation.

HUMAN RIGHTS

In Catholic social teaching this economic minimum which is owed to every person by society is made explicit by a specific set of economic rights — for example, the right to adequate income, the right to employment, food, shelter, medical care, education, etc. These fundamental personal rights form a kind of baseline, a set of minimum conditions for economic justice. They form a bottom line for judging how well economic institutions are protecting human dignity and promoting social solidarity.

Our discussion of these economic rights takes place in a society that understands political rights but questions the very idea of economic rights. Therefore, we call for the formation of a new cultural consensus that all persons really do have rights in the economic sphere and that society has a moral obligation to take the necessary steps to ensure that no one among us is hungry, homeless, unemployed, or otherwise denied what is necessary to live with dignity.

GLOBAL INTERDEPENDENCE

The interdependence of our nation with the rest of the world is very evident when one examines the American economy. Whether the issue is employment, trade policy, monetary policy, or virtually any other major economic issue, there is growing and inescapable connection between our nation's economic decisions and fortunes and those of the rest of the world. But this interdependence must be viewed in a broader sense than just economic. There is also a moral interdependence that extends beyond our national boundaries. We are a single moral community at the global level. Therefore, the fact that 800 million people in the world live in absolute poverty and nearly half a billion persons are chronically hungry is not irrelevant to our search for just economic policies. In the pastoral letter we suggest that the option for the poor be used as a general moral framework with which to view the international economy. Such a perspective suggests that we give high priority to north-south issues such as third-world debt that threaten the futures of some of the poor nations.

CONCLUSION

We know we cannot be true to our religious heritage and be silent on the question of economic justice. We need people who can find the moral in the midst of the human, people who are committed to the best of our tradition of liberty and justice for all. It is our hope that by calling explicit attention to the moral dimensions of economic decision making, we in the Church can contribute to the achievement of an economy that is both healthy and just, that is both dynamic and fair, that respects the freedom of the human person but also protects the rights of the weak and the poor.

I commend the committee for convening this symposium to mark the 40th anniversary of the committee and the Employment Act of 1946. One of your stated goals for this event is to review what we have learned from the past 40 years. I hope that we have learned that economic decisions are also moral and political decisions. As we struggle to meet the new challenges posed by the changing economy, let us not forget that these complex questions are ultimately about human beings and human values.

CHAPTER 9

How to Read the Economic Pastoral

There is much talk these days about the relationship between religion and society, between faith and politics, between the Church and the world.[1] Within the Catholic Church this debate often centers around how one interprets the documents of the Second Vatican Council. Cardinal Joseph Ratzinger, Prefect of the Congregation for the Doctrine of the Faith of the Roman Curia, has called, for example, for a kind of new withdrawal from the world, a new *fuga mundi*. In the book *The Ratzinger Report*, in terms that sound much like the Fathers of the Patristic period, he has challenged the Catholic Church to take a stance of opposition against the modern world.[2] The bishops gathered at Vatican Council II grappled with that question and came out with a different solution in their document *The Pastoral Constitution on the Church in the Modern World* (*Gaudium et spes*). In paragraphs 40–45 of that document, a more nuanced vision of the way in which the earthly city and the heavenly city compenetrate each other is given. There it is stated that the Church, acting through her individual members and her whole community, believes she can contbute greatly toward making our world and our history more human. In positive terms, then, that document states the following:

> With great respect, therefore, this council regards all the true, good and just elements inherent in the very wide variety of institutions which the human race has established for itself and constantly continues to establish. This council affirms, moreover, that the Church is willing to assist and promote all these institutions to the extent that such a service depends on her and can be associated with her mission.[3]

VATICAN II AND ECONOMIC ISSUES

Among those institutions in which the Church interacts, one should also mention the economic arrangements that are integral to any society. The relationship between Church and world and all these institutions, moreover, is seen as a two-way street in which the Church profits much from the world and is enriched by human social life and development.

The second half of that conciliar document deals with several specific subjects. Chapter 3 is devoted entirely to economic and social life. That chapter ends with the following admonition: "Christians who take an active part in present-day socio-economic development and fight for justice and charity should be convinced that they can make a great contribution to the prosperity of humankind and to the peace of the world."[4] This document, promulgated in 1965, remains the source of much that is in the Economic Pastoral Letter of the American bishops and is the theological backdrop for it.

Perhaps no other sentence in that document clarifies the perspectives of the Economic Pastoral Letter more succinctly than this one:

> Pursuing the saving purpose which is proper to her, the Church does not only communicate divine life over to human beings but in some way casts the reflected light of that life over the entire earth, most of all by its healing and elevating impact on the dignity of the person, by the way in which it strengthens the seams of human society and imbues the everyday activity of people with a deeper meaning and importance.[5]

As one can see, those aspects of life that touch on the dignity of the person and the quality of human life are also of importance to the faith. For us in the U.S. the separation of Church and state cannot be interpreted to mean that there is a separation of economic issues from religious issues, but rather that we must have a concern for all those socioeconomic issues that touch the quality of human life. We have expressed this by saying that we are concerned by what an economic system does to people and for people and how it permits people to participate in it. In a pluralistic society we are indeed interested in how these issues are discussed in the public forum and want to contribute our reflections based on our particular faith tradition.

The sources of our teaching are twofold: the Bible and Catholic social teaching. Before the Second Vatican Council one could have begun a document such as the Economic Pastoral Letter without much reference to sacred scripture. Today that would be impossible, since our people have become more and more a biblical people. The change of the liturgy to the vernacular has made Catholics more acquainted with scripture, our priests preach more and more on the basis of scriptural texts, our theologians base their reflections on scriptural sources. Moreover, we find for this topic of economic arrangements much inspiration in the Hebrew scriptures. Perhaps no other document from the Catholic Church in recent memory has been inspired so much by the Old Testament tradition.

Our second source is Catholic social teaching. The paragraphs mentioned in the document of Vatican Council II on *The Church in the Modern World* that dealt with economic life did not come out of nowhere, but represent the thinking of a consistent body of teaching that goes back to the last century. Pope Leo XIII was the first to wrestle with the relationship between the Catholic tradition and the new industrial age. Much of the social teaching of the Middle Ages had been lost or seemed irrelevant in the light of subsequent socioeconomic conditions. But the plight of the worker during the nineteenth century and the rise of statism and collectivism forced Leo to reflect on the rights of workers and the need to say something about those rights in relationship to the state and society. Starting in 1891 — a bit late, it is true — there has been in the Catholic Church a tradition of reflecting on socioeconomic issues. Much of that tradition was not based on scripture but on natural-law philosophies. Our present Pope and his two immediate predecessors, Pope John XXIII and Pope Paul VI, have spoken and written much out of that tradition. Paragraphs such as those quoted from the Second Vatican Council would have been impossible without that body of teaching. We see our own Economic Pastoral Letter as coming out of that tradition, of being true to it, but of moving further in analyzing it and bringing it into sharper focus. We have complemented this tradition with more biblical sources, but we have also appreciated the depth of the philosophical thought that is inherent in it. Especially in our dialogue with the ecumenical community, we have appreciated how helpful it has been to use the truths of philosophy and science in passing from a scriptural vision to present-day phenomena.

METHODOLOGY

Our methodology has been to write the letter, as it were, in public. We began with a long series of hearings in an attempt to grapple with the topic in a realistic way and to hear from all sectors of society and from all points of view. In the light of that knowledge we tried to formulate from sacred scripture and from Catholic social teaching those visions and truths that would help us. We were seeking guidance on how economic decision making and the moral values we hold intersect. We made no attempt to repeat the whole of Catholic social teaching but enunciated only those ideas and principles that affected the theme assigned us. These principles we attempted to lay out in order. In this section the debate on the first draft centered more on the ethical norms than on the biblical vision and we were thus able to clarify them in the second draft. Since this is the "centerpiece" of the document, we continued our reflections into the third draft. For most readers it is the most difficult section, but it remains the key for understanding the whole letter.

Our process has also been highly ecumenical. In selecting presenters at the closed hearings, we were interested in obtaining the best experts in the area of concern, without regard to faith affiliation. We also held special hearings arranged for us by the non-Catholic and Jewish communities. We felt that it was imperative to obtain this ecumenical input before the writing of the first draft because of the valuable contribution we saw this to be.

In the middle of our work on the first draft, there rose a controversy about the teaching authority of a conference of bishops. It was not the role of our committee to solve such an ecclesiological problem. We counted on a certain level of sophistication on the part of our readers to differentiate among the levels of material we are dealing with. Thus, we write:

> Throughout this letter, when we treat the fundamentals of Christian faith, Church teaching, and basic moral principles, we are proposing norms which should inform the consciences of the members of our Church. When we make recommendations about specific decisions or policies in the economic sphere, we recognize that prudential judgments are involved. These depend on the accuracy of our facts and on our assessment of them. Although we believe these judgments are correct and will stand up to public scrutiny, we acknowledge that differing conclusions are possible even among those who share the same moral objectives. From Catholics and from others we expect and welcome debate on these more specific conclusions.[6]

It would be impossible to take each statement in such a lengthy letter and try to assess its authoritative value. We are aware of the fact that there is often a gap between the intent willed and the outcome in reality. Social theorists must deal with this phenomenon constantly. The more rapidly an economy is changing, the more difficult it is to harness it and to control its effects. Thus a gap can exist between principle and policy. Often, too, the vision proposed seems to be "utopian," in that it demands the striving for the alleviation of all evils or inadequacies. The reality often means a certain compromise because of the inability of a society to do all things at once. Thus one could hold that certain principles can only be put into full operation after other matters have been taken care of. The problem of the deficit is such an issue. On the other hand, to have no vision and no goals or to resign oneself to the status quo without positive steps to arrive at the ends desired is in itself morally untenable. In our pluralistic society a compromise in implementation does not imply always a compromise in principle.

CONTENTS OF THE ECONOMIC PASTORAL LETTER

After this first section on preliminary subjects, so that the economic pastoral letter can be put into its proper perspective, I would like to comment on the contents of the letter as an aid to reading it more easily.

Since most Americans are accustomed to inductive reasoning processes, they found the first draft to be too deductive—that is, too concerned with principles to be applied. We decided in the second draft to present the material in a slightly different fashion in order to lay out the questions in a more inductive fashion before going on to principles. The first chapter attempts to show the average reader the importance of the subject of relating economic decision making with the daily task of living in society. Not all the questions raised in this chapter could be treated later in the letter, but it attempts to be a survey of the situation of the domestic and international economic scene and the positive and negative effects that system is producing on this world. It is necessarily too short and must presuppose that the reader has some acquaintance with the questions raised. Perhaps our first revelation as a committee was that the general population does not possess such knowledge and that there is an urgent need for more general understanding of the economic picture of the world. The fact, however, that this letter raised such an enormous discussion in all circles of our population shows that there is a genuine interest in trying to grapple with these issues in an intelligent and systematic fashion. There is also a felt need not only to understand what is happening but also to bring to this arena a sense of direction and an understanding of the values projected.

In the introduction we have emphasized as the new moment or the special sign of our times the interdependency of nations in the economic sphere. Nations have always traded and relied on one another, but the way in which the nations of the world are tied together economically at this moment of history has no precedent. It has caused the failure of older methods of economic analysis to function as before; it has occasioned the rethinking of many time-honored principles that have previously worked. It will continue to vex the theoreticians. We know that we wrote our letter at this crucial moment when the reality of a world economy is forming. It is a good time to reflect on what is happening and what the future of the globe might look like.

We know that it is also an important moment because of the constant tension between east and west and the economic consequences of this tension for the whole world. From the feedback we have received from third-world nations, we have come to realize the importance of this controversy for them in their search for resolutions to economic problems. We sense a need to present values to our economic system that go beyond the profit motive, that are in accord with religious belief, and that respond to the desires and yearnings of so many on this globe. We see our document as a contribution to that attempt, and it has been recognized as such by many in the third world. This ideological struggle is real to the Catholic Church and within the Catholic Church, and we find ourselves in the middle of it because of historical events. We are forced, as members of this nation that is seen as the leader and example of capitalism, to examine the values of our society and to articulate how they resonate with our Catholic faith. Our failure to do so at this moment would be an omission that could have grave consequences. I hope that our letter will continue to bring us as a Church closer to the people of the third world, so that we can see better the relationships between our economies and can also articulate the concerns not only of our own citizens but also of the citizens of other countries affected by our economy. The feedback from the first draft has made us aware of the enormity of the task but also of its timeliness.

One should not seek in the Bible practical solutions to complex socio-economic problems of today. But the Bible does have something to say about how people should relate to one another. It has something to say about the value of people and the importance of life and how life should be lived. Our document reflects on the Genesis story, for example, to search out the place of the human person in the act of creation. From the account it is clear that the sacred writer sees the human person as the peak of creation, that the human person is made to the image and likeness of God and is given a kind of control over creation. Such a dignity we affirm precedes race or national boundaries. Here the biblical vision coincides with the philosophical assertions that the dignity of the person is manifest in the ability that humans have to reason and understand, which forms the basis of their freedom to shape their lives and the life of their communities.

We all are aware, however, that this human dignity must be lived out in communion with others in society. That primary social concept is exemplified in the history of the Jewish people of old. God made a covenant with them as his people. He outlined for them how they were to live in relationship one to another in fulfillment of that covenant. The message of Jesus takes those concepts further toward that universalism that is inherent in them. Love and solidarity extend beyond national borders (for example, the story of the Good Samaritan), to all. We state, thus: "The commandment to love God with all one's heart and to love one's neighbor as oneself are the heart and soul of Christian morality." Within that concept of solidarity with others lie also the duties and rights of each member of society. We speak of the requirements of justice in community and the duties and obligations of the community's members. Within that section on justice we present the traditional Catholic social teaching on distributive justice and the need to be concerned about those whose basic material needs are not met. The term that has become classic now in contemporary literature is the "preferential option for the poor." Perhaps one should just say: "the clear choice to come to the aid of the poor." The biblical vision stressed this concept in its own way. As a part of the covenant between God and his people, special care for those without political right and power was prescribed: the widows, the orphans, and the aliens or strangers in the land. If there is any revolutionary aspect of Christ's teaching, it is clearly in his attitude toward the poor. In the Sermon on the Mount, when he told the poor that every hair on their heads was numbered because of their worth in the eyes of their heavenly Father, he was again emphasizing this dignity of each person and the special role each has in society.

Within the same context we reiterate the teaching of recent Popes on the question of economic rights. If one has a right to life, one has a right to all that is needed to sustain life. This concept will require continued discussion on our part but may well become even more important than it now seems to be. The whole of society guarantees these rights. As we move toward more automation, as our job market changes in the types of people needed for the jobs created, we may find this concept of even more value in determining a just society. Neo-Malthusianism is not foreign to our day. We are saying that all have a right to contribute to the common good, and we make the fulfillment of the basic needs of the poor the highest priority of any society.

These concepts of solidarity and the way in which human dignity is lived out in society have led to a further concept in Catholic social teaching, *subsidiarity*. It is a concept that is meant to place limits on the role of government. Father John Pawlikowski, O.S.M., describes it this way:

> The principle holds that it is a serious violation of just social order to allow larger political entities to absorb functions that smaller and lower communities can ably carry out. Subsidiarity assigns to the State the responsibility of assisting in the empowerment of smaller groups. The State must not destroy these groups nor interfere with their operations.[7]

There seem to be no biblical roots for this concept, but it rose out of the theological and political need to guarantee freedom to institutional pluralism, initiative, and creativity. It does not deny the need for global structures to correspond to the dynamics of our present economy, nor does it state that the government that governs least governs best. It simply tries to protect freedom and to delineate roles in such a way as to safeguard that freedom.

We have complemented this section on ethical norms with a section on the economic actors needed in any society. Here we deal with workers and labor unions, owners and managers, citizens and government. Pope John Paul II has caused a rethinking in this area with his 1981 encyclical, *Laborem exercens*. He takes workers or labor in an inclusive sense, to embrace management. His now-famous dictum of "labor over capital" is simply a reminder that the economy is meant for people and they are to be its controllers and subject, not to be its object and to be manipulated by it. In that encyclical he also restated the position of Catholic social teaching on private property or ownership by again defending the right to private ownership but insisting that it is not an absolute or unconditioned right. He places the common good above this right and calls it the value that regulates it. Some feel that this section is not challenging enough. It does sound a bit theoretical, since it deals primarily with principles that tend to be abstract. Some also wished that we had emphasized more the

distinct vocation of the laity here and spelled out more clearly the consequences of these principles on the lives of each person. That would have
taken a full book. Perhaps in subsequent writings we can make this section
more challenging and more practical.

We summarize the vision of this whole biblical and ethical section as
follows:

> Every human person is created as an image of God, and the denial
> of dignity to a person is a blot on this image. Creation is a gift to all
> men and women, not to be appropriated for the benefit of a few; its
> beauty is an object of joy and reverence. The same God who came to
> the aid of an oppressed people and formed them into a covenant
> community continues to hear the cries of the oppressed and to create
> communities which are to hear his word. God's love and life are
> present when people can live in a community of faith and hope. These
> cardinal points of the faith of Israel also furnish the religious context
> for understanding the saving action of God in the life and teaching
> of Jesus.[8]

Many bishops had asked the committee to clarify where our document
stands concerning systemic economic issues, that is, how we view capitalism,
as such. It was not a request for a theoretical analysis of capitalism but
rather a statement of position. We do this before chapter 3 of the second
draft as an introduction to the policy section. It is clear that our document
is one of a "mixed" economy, one that is not afraid of alterations in the
unfettered free-market system to obtain the greatest benefit of all. It is not
a "third way" or a specific new economic system; that is not our purpose.
We feel it has been in the very best U.S. tradition to continue to search
for an ever-more-just economy.

SPECIFICITY AND THE BISHOPS

Many bishops also asked us to be careful in this section of policy application, lest we become too specific. It would have to be admitted that the
hardest task before our committee was the degree of specificity with which
the body of bishops would be at ease. It seems that the second draft was
within the range that they desired.

One question that arose constantly in the feedback was the role of government in dealing with specific issues. Here the replies from all sectors of
society seemed to respond to concerns according to party affiliation. We
were aware of the fact that the role of government in Catholic social teaching is a more positive one than that currently in vogue around the nation.
There is no hint in Catholic social teaching of the forms of libertarian
philosophy that one finds on the rise today in U.S. society. I suppose this
strain has been a part of capitalism since the days of mercantilism, but it

is not found in the concepts on government that characterized medieval philosophy and thus did not become a part of classic Catholic theory. We tried to point out this more positive role of government in our first section, but there remains a need for a fuller treatment. In an article entitled "John Courtney Murray and the Pastoral Letters" (*America*, Nov. 30, 1985), John A. Rohr argues that the economic pastoral would not be acceptable to Father John Courtney Murray, S.J., if he were alive, because it does not take government seriously. He would have begun, the author states, with the nature of government and reasoned from there. Our document does take government seriously—more seriously than we feel many of the respondents do—but we did not want to do a treatise on the role of government in order to do one on the economy. Nevertheless, many questions are left unanswered and will require further thought on our part.

From an economic point of view, serious questions are also raised by the economic phenomenon we see today. The U.S. must compete against many nations that sustain their economies in different ways than our own, that subsidize and plan in ways that we do not support, and that carry on experiments for national businesses to give them a world edge. These questions more rightly belong to the economists to debate, but they presuppose a position on how government and business should relate. I look forward to continued discussion on the role of government.

THE POLICY SECTION

When the committee had completed the theoretical section, it debated long on the need to enter into policy suggestions and, if so, how to do it. After much thought it was felt necessary to enter into this type of reasoning so that the theory would not end in midair, but become the source for policy seeking. Then the discussion centered on what themes to pick for these policy demonstrations. We finally settled on 5 out of a possible 26 that were suggested by committee members. In the second draft the number is four: employment, poverty, agriculture, and third-world trade and aid. These four do not make a complete economic or moral analysis; they are but a beginning, and must be seen as such.

Our presentations of employment and poverty overlap and have engendered much discussion in the nation. Perhaps the most trenchant criticism was that the solutions proposed seemed to repeat the already discarded programs of the war against poverty or the programs of "The Great Society." Many political elements are mixed into this economic criticism, but I feel that the months of debate have been helpful. Almost all today recognize that poverty is still very real among us and that the rate of unemployment—very much related to the poverty question—has not dropped to a sufficient level. There is perhaps a certain frustration. Many are aware of the problem but do not feel that much can be done about it. It is certainly true that just throwing money at it—as some describe the Great Society programs—is no answer. It is not at all proven to our satisfaction that the welfare programs of the Great Society are the cause of the present intractable situation. The number of people who go in and out of poverty, who want to work, is too large for such a facile solution.

We do feel that positive solutions are open to us today. In addition to the creation of new jobs to reduce the unemployment rate (we feel that a collaborative effort in this respect between government and the private sector would be helpful), we see other positive signs from programs tried and from new ones now suggested. We know that these will be costly, that they will be best put into practice with as much subsidiarity as possible and with as little bureaucracy as needed. Naturally, we are most concerned about strengthening our educational system. One can talk much about incentives, but the most effective incentives come with quality education. Education is also the source of the skills needed for jobs today. Many other questions require not so much economic solutions but solutions where both the economic and the psychological aspects are carefully analyzed to bring some clarity to the problems. Recent articles and experiments show hope in those areas. I might add that I feel religion is and should be one of the prime forces in giving people a sense of dignity and worth and helping them to see their role and duties in society. Perhaps the challenge to religion in this area is only now becoming evident.

The agriculture section has been especially difficult. An immediate crisis is at hand, and we have a mind-set about such problems that go back to Jefferson and the founding of the nation. It has been most difficult to seek solutions to the current problems and at the same time to take a long-term look at the whole question of food supply around the globe. More radical solutions will have to be devised in the future, but I am not sure that we have the political will to face them. I regret in this study that economists did not follow through on some of the research of early capitalist theorists who dealt specifically with natural resources and land as special in an economic system because they are fundamental for the subsistence of people. They present special problems that cannot be so easily resolved. We raise some of these issues but do not go into them in depth. Perhaps those who cry for a more limited government involvement should also clarify where they stand on the phenomenon of the large tracts of land and resources that are government owned. Catholic social teaching grew out of the Industrial Revolution and has always had an urban imprint. It, too, needs a more profound analysis of these questions. In some respects one could say that the agriculture chapter of the document is still far from finished. It will remain the subject of much debate for years to come.

The separate section on the United States and the world economy is too short for such a complicated subject, and it has received the least amount of feedback. That is unfortunate, as it is a key chapter and one that means much for the future. Because of the signs of the times and the economic interdependency mentioned in the first chapter, this discussion is important to the whole edifice. The small feedback probably represents the lack of knowledge on the part of most Americans in this complicated subject. To many, the terms used and the international institutions mentioned were all foreign concepts. The only consistent criticism that we received from the third world—and this criticism came primarily from American missionaries abroad—was that we were too lenient in describing the effects of multinationals on third-world life and financial crises. Many wanted us to take a specific stand condemning multinationals, but we felt that this was not in order. A history of the behavior of multinationals would have to be accompanied by a history of the behavior of the host nations and many elements in them, as well. This did not seem to be a profitable course for us to pursue.

We are aware, however, that here and in other places of our document we seem to be naive about the extent of power that accompanies such large economic institutions. The relationship between power and money is one that we did not avoid, but it is true that we failed to give it the significance it deserves. Many of the members of the committee would have liked to have seen this section much larger and more detailed, but as a beginning it seems to be adequate. Perhaps the hearings we have had with third-world economists and the feedback from the second draft will help us formulate this section in a more cogent way. Perhaps, too, with time our people will become more acquainted with this whole area and be more inclined to respond to the ideas presented. It is one thing to talk about a global economy; it is another thing to realize all the ramifications of that concept.

OTHER THEMES

In all of these questions several themes recurred among the respondents. The first deals with the family. There was a general concern that we did not treat sufficiently of the effects of our economic system on the family. I will admit that it is difficult to be clear on what is cause and what is effect in this area. The large numbers of women entering the work force in recent years is connected with this issue, but it is not easy to state without error what this fact means in terms of the family and family life. It is easier to treat the phenomenon of so many single-parent households due to divorce or the lack of a father. Even here there are deeper sociological causes that are at work, and one would not want to be simplistic in giving solutions or be moralistic in denouncing trends that might have other causes at their roots.

Many want more analysis of the effects of the military buildup on the economy. On this subject we have inserted much more in the second draft than in the first but have shied away from a full treatment. Although we have examined some of the studies done on the possible conversion from military to a full capitalist use of money, and although we have explicitly stated that we feel a reduction in military spending is called for so that the social programs which we see as absolutely necessary today can be carried out, we do not treat at great length the whole military question and the economy. I doubt that our third draft will be able to do much more than the second has done in this regard. We have been explicit about the sale of arms and have deplored the fact that so many third-world nations spend so much to obtain arms when vital human needs are not being fulfilled. These questions become political and are not solved by economic means alone.

Some have found our treatment insufficient in terms of economic trade-offs needed to take care of the social problems of today. Some very urgent contemporary questions were not treated, such as the deficit, which require solution before any of the other questions we raised can be treated. In response I would have to say we do not consider these as either-or situations, but it is true that a new listing of priorities would have to be effected to find solutions to problems we consider more urgent. Much of the economic material we gathered in this area we felt should not be placed in our document, as it would be too specific for a moral treatise coming from the mouths of bishops who are not professional economists. We also had to admit that the present state of economic analysis would mean the presentation of many theories, not all as yet very conclusive. In some respects we took the easier road of stating objectives to be aimed at rather than specific solutions. We are hoping that this kind of discussion will continue among professional economists and are happy to see that our document is indeed stimulating such research.

It is true that we at first tried to examine the whole question of planning and the economy. This proved to be a word that caused so much confusion that we have only briefly referred to it. Instead, we see the future as presenting a broader challenge of new forms of collaboration and cooperation that are only now in their incipient stage. At first these forms look innocent enough and are already being tried in the U.S. and elsewhere. A closer look at this section, chapter 4, shows that more is at stake. People are becoming more and more aware that there is a shift of political power taking place because of the strength and importance of large corporate economic undertakings. People are noticing that with these new international and multinational firms goes also much power that can only be called political. It is also becoming more evident that people want more control over the economic decisions that affect their lives even though it does not involve such large international holdings. At first we used the term "economic democracy," but then felt that such a term carried with it a certain amount of intellectual baggage and was best avoided. The concept, however, remains. Pope John Paul II, in the encyclical *Laborem exercens*, enlarged the concept of participation in the workplace to include more democratic participation by workers in economic decisions that affect their lives. Paragraph 285 sums up our reasons for writing this chapter:

The nation's founders took daring steps to create structures of mutual accountability and widely distributed power to ensure that the political system would support the rights and freedoms of all. We believe that similar institutional steps are needed today to expand the sharing of economic power and to relate the economic system more accountably to the common good. Since there is no single innovation that will solve all problems, we recommend careful experimentation with several possibilities that hold considerable hope for increasing partnership and strengthening mutual responsibility for economic justice.[9]

I might mention that perhaps this chapter, little discussed in the press and little commented on by individual respondents, might contain within it much that will indicate future trends and prove to be more prophetic than perhaps even the authors foresee.

We look forward now to digesting the feedback on this second draft and to redoing the document one more time. The final vote on that third and final draft will take place among the bishops next November (1986). Although it will be a final draft of this letter, it will not mean an end to the fascinating and important search for ways and means of making our economy and the world economy more equitable and more just. In so many ways we feel we are only at the beginning of reflecting on how our faith and the values that flow from it intersect with the economic realities we live under. That kind of reflection, I hope, will never end.

CHAPTER 10

Economic Justice and
the American Tradition

INTRODUCTION

In November of 1980 the bishops of the United States, gathered at their annual meeting, decided to write two pastoral letters: one on the whole question of the nuclear buildup and its moral implications, and another on capitalism and Christianity.[1] Both letters proceeded simultaneously, but the urgency of the subject matter concerning the nuclear buildup took precedence, and that pastoral letter was debated and voted upon before the completion of the second letter. The second letter began as a more theoretical analysis of the relationship between capitalism as an economic system and the biblical and natural-law traditions of Roman Catholic morality. It was soon discovered that this theoretical approach would be most difficult for a pastoral letter. Although there was abundant literature on the relationship between various Christian bodies and capitalism, especially the relationship between Presbyterianism and capitalism, it was felt that this approach would be too highly academic and would not be of help to the Catholic population of the United States.

After many hearings around the nation and much discussion, the committee of five bishops decided to limit the topic to an analysis of the contemporary economic system of the United States and its relationship to Catholic social teaching. From the very beginning it was stated by all the members of the committee that this limitation had many drawbacks. Some believed that it was absolutely imperative to deal with the American economy in terms of the global economy from the very beginning. On the other hand, it was also realized that, although this perspective could be kept in mind, it would not be possible to deal with the relationship of the United States' economy to the entire world at this time. It was also felt that it would not be fruitful for the Catholic population of the United States to undergo a complete analysis of the various economic theories that are now

108

current in our universities and the business community because they are so divergent that a complete analysis would entail many, many volumes.

The bishops instead decided that it would be necessary to deal with the effects the economy was having on the lives of the people of the nation and begin with that kind of more phenomenological approach. In doing so they realized the limitations of the letter and in subsequent drafts tried to rectify that set of weaknesses by including more and more materials that dealt with systemic analysis. Many philosophical and economic issues simply seemed outside the purview of such a letter because of their technical specificity.

The letter thus begins with an analysis of the present state of affairs, emphasizing not only the domestic but also the global issues that must be faced. It points out, in particular, the need for a moral vision for the whole of society, if the various specialized groups of society are to work together toward a common good.

Because of the lack in the United States of an awareness of Catholic social teaching, it was also necessary to cull from that teaching those principles which affect the economy and, in particular, the economic situation of the United States. It was also necessary to relate that teaching, based as it is mostly on natural law, to the biblical vision that is so fundamental to our Christian tradition.

The bishops felt, having reached this point, that it would also be necessary to deal with several concrete examples to show the American Catholic population how the principles from the biblical and ethical vision affect daily life and the economic decisions of both nation and individuals. A certain danger was immediately recognized in this kind of application because of the contingencies involved, because of the rapidly changing economic factors, and because of the difficulty in arriving at concrete options. Nevertheless, it was felt necessary to touch these examples. It was realized also that the American mentality is highly inductive and must begin with the concrete in order to understand what the principles are all about.

The principles of chapter 2 became very important in analyzing this situation in the U.S.A. and the whole question of the relationship between our industrialized world and the third world, with its huge debts. There was no opportunity to deal with the relationship between the U.S. economy and developed nations, such as West Germany or Japan, and this was indeed regrettable, but it was impossible to deal with all aspects of the question of economic relationships in a global economy. The bishops knew that many of the elements that they could not take up would have to be dealt with subsequently, especially by specialists. They hoped that the examples given would stimulate the continued debate on the issues presented, as well as many more, in the light of Catholic social teaching.

It seemed necessary in the pastoral letter to also talk about who makes economic decisions. Thus a chapter was added about new kinds of cooperation and collaboration that could help alter some of the present situations that seem to be so unjust and leave no choice to the worker. This chapter spells out new ways of economic decision making that are more collaborative than in the past.

Finally, the document had to deal with the inner life of the Church itself. Here the bishops wanted to point out the relationship between economic decisions and leisure and also between the reading of the scripture at liturgy and how this affects the conscience of the individual Catholic. It also had to emphasize the relationship between liturgy and the forming of a community-based ethos in the population. The Church was also called upon to examine its own economic practices, and a series of questions was posed to it, to make sure that the internal justice dimension is not lacking within the Church. This call to the members of the Church is not seen just as an institutional question but also as a call to each individual Catholic to assume his or her role in the marketplace and thus have an influence on the kind of decisions that will be more just for the entire society.

After this brief outline of the contents of the letter, I would like to say a word about the pastoral message that precedes it. This message was the result of much debate on the floor among the bishops, who felt that the pastoral letter had to be excessively long to cover all of the points requested. The pastoral message is meant to be a brief summary of the letter but at the same time intends to be exhortatory and encourage the Catholic population to study the letter and become acquainted with its contents. It is not meant as a substitute for the letter but rather as a summary and introduction to it.

After this brief analysis of the contents of the letter, I would like to place the letter in various contexts in order to explain better how it came into being and what thoughts often lie behind it that are not and cannot be totally expressed in the letter. Most of all, it must be emphasized that it comes out of a U.S.A. context at this moment of history and must be seen as a pastoral letter in the light of that situation.

ECCLESIAL CONTEXT

A pastoral letter is seen primarily as a teaching document of a conference of bishops. It is not intended to be either too simple or too academic in tone. The style of the pastoral letters in the past in the United States has been consistently didactic. Because of the general educational climate in the United States, it was foreseen from the beginning that other educational tools would have to be prepared to accompany such a letter: audiovisual presentations, digests, discussion questions, and the like. Nevertheless, the bishops decided that such longer letters are important because they permit one to spell out more clearly what the concepts involved mean and do not limit one to a more superficial popularization. They give a clear backdrop for the other educational tools.

Probably the most important question is the audience to whom the letter is addressed. Primarily the audience of such a letter is the Catholic population of the United States. It is important to realize that population has changed dramatically since the Second World War. Before that time the Church considered itself mostly as composed of immigrants who were among the class of unskilled laborers. It was rare to find a Catholic in the higher echelons of big business or politics. After the Second World War many Catholic families took advantage of the grants for higher education that came from the GI bills and began to attend some of the most prestigious universities of the nation. Within a few decades after the war, the Catholic population could be found entering into the upper classes of business and government, so that by 1980 it was quite common for Catholics to be found in all the different branches of society in increasingly large numbers. For these reasons the Economic Pastoral Letter addresses a different audience than any of the statements of the American bishops before the Second World War. Its audience now must be Catholics in all strata of society.

One of the most important aspects of the letter in its ecclesial context was certainly the process whereby three drafts were produced and the Catholic population of the United States was permitted to react to and respond to those three drafts. The lengthy hearings before even the first draft was written permitted the academic, political, and business communities to have their share of input, in addition to permitting the poor and those who were adversely affected by the economy to have their voices heard. That process has been much talked about and analyzed, but one could say that the document could never have been done without it. Listening to those who were involved was absolutely important; the hearings helped delineate the questions to be asked and select out the most important economic issues facing the nation.

One of the most difficult questions concerning the genre of the pastoral letter was the degree of specificity with which it should treat subjects. After the first draft, there was much debate among the bishops concerning the question of specificity. It seemed that the bishops were a bit uneasy with too many concrete statistics and felt that the role of the teaching authority was indeed to put forth the principles and even to go beyond them to present descriptive norms, but not to descend into that which would be too specific. This process was not always easy to follow in practice, but it did remain a more or less general principle in the writing of the letter.

However, probably the most important contribution that the letter makes in the ecclesial context is indeed the process used and the way in which a teaching Church has discerned what is consonant with Catholic teaching among the many voices in a society. It also witnessed to the fact that the laity does have a most important role to play in that process and felt very much a part of the teaching dynamics within the Church. The bishops on the committee at no time felt that their teaching roles were being minimized by the process involved. They realized it was their duty to discern where the truth lay and to present this to the full body of bishops. The full body of bishops treated the letter in that fashion and modified it with amendments which they felt would make the teaching clearer and more precise. The final vote of the bishops indicated clearly that the process had been most effective for arriving at a consensus among the bishops as to the way in which economic decisions and Catholic social teaching intersect.

THEOLOGICAL CONTEXT

One of the most trying questions that the committee had to deal with was the relationship between the biblical vision and the natural-law ethic that permeates Catholic social teaching. At first the tendency on the part of the committee was to draw these two together into a single section. After much discussion and debate, it was felt that it might be wise in the present U.S. context to leave the two sections separate.

The biblical vision is most important for the Catholic population at this point of history and had to necessarily precede the natural-law section and be dealt with at greater length. The questions posed by the biblical section were integral to the entire document. The treatise of human dignity in solidarity, as found in the Old Testament, seemed to be the entire document in outline. The several drafts of the document saw a sharper focus on New Testament thinking to complement the section on the Old Testament, as well as a tendency to relate this again to contemporary thought.

Since the Second Vatican Council, the Catholic population of the United States has become much more aware of the importance of the biblical vision, not only in their daily lives but in their whole thinking process. This acquaintance with the Bible has transformed much of U.S. Catholicism in recent decades. It perhaps is also the source of some of the apparent divisions in Catholic thinking. Because the pastoral letter would be used outside the Catholic Church and become a part of the whole political debate in the nation, it was felt useful to leave the arguments that were based more on natural-law theories as a separate section.

It was felt that many people in the United States would be in agreement with the principles of this section, even though they would not hold the same Catholic faith that we do. In the debate that followed the various drafts, it was seen that this distinction was not that important and that one could have proceeded in other fashions. Nevertheless, given the tensions in the United States over the way in which religion should relate to political issues, it has been most helpful to present those issues also from their philosophical, not just their Catholic or religious, point of view. This has minimized some of the tension and helped in having the document accepted by a wider audience than just those who follow the Catholic faith.

Much remains to be done yet on how that biblical vision intertwines with so many of the natural-law theories upon which Catholic social teaching is based. A complete unity of those two sections has not yet been done by

Catholic moralists throughout the world. One could say that the Economic Pastoral Letter of the bishops represents at this point of history the best effort that has been done toward such a reconciliation but that the results are not totally satisfying and complete.

In writing the Economic Pastoral Letter, the bishops were also well aware of the fact that Catholic social teaching is not a static concept. It has accepted the historical progress within that teaching. Thus the bishops accepted a certain growth in Catholic social teaching and hoped that the Economic Pastoral Letter would contribute to that growth.

One of the first contributions has already been mentioned, namely, a deeper analysis of the biblical vision that must support, underlie, and coincide with the natural-law principles that have been a part of the historical approach to Catholic social teaching. It has acknowledged also the changes in emphasis that have occurred throughout history, from *Rerum novarum* to *Laborem exercens*. For example, it has accepted without question the interpretation of private property as given in the document *Laborem exercens* by Pope John Paul II, which modifies and makes much more Thomistic the concepts found in *Rerum novarum*. It has certainly accepted fully the implications of the international aspects of economic justice as found in *Pacem in terris*; in fact, one could say that it sees that document as a certain turning point in Catholic social teaching, because from then on all aspects of economic justice have a global significance and a global context.

One of the concepts that was much discussed in the United States with the appearance of the letter was the concept of solidarity. Many objected to the word, and there has been much debate as to how the word should be used in Catholic social teaching. It was necessary to emphasize for the U.S. population the way in which the human person fulfills himself or herself within society and the need today to stress the importance of the common good. Those aspects of the document have forced some rather conservative critics to label the document socialistic, although this is certainly not the intent of the bishops in the use of the word *solidarity*. The word is now becoming more acceptable in the U.S. context, especially after recent discussion on the meaning of the concept of the common good.

One could say that the Economic Pastoral Letter has not added anything to the already existing doctrines on common good that were expressed especially by Pope John XXIII. However, the way in which the document describes the concept of preferential option for the poor under the concept of common good is indeed a progression in Catholic social thought. Many objected to the use of the term "preferential option for the poor" because of its use in liberation theology, but it was felt by the committee that this term has a deep biblical root and could be well established philosophically within the natural-law tradition as a subsection under the common good. Whenever any group is excluded from participating fully in the goods of society, one can say that the common good is indeed harmed. It has been noticed subsequently that the acceptance of such an interpretation has been without difficulty. It has also differentiated itself from some of the other philosophical theories that are prevalent in the United States and especially in the academic community, such as the writings of John Rawls.

One of the more interesting aspects of the Economic Pastoral Letter has been the insertion of the concept of economic rights into this moral section. The debate that surrounded this introduction on the part of the drafting committee centered mostly on who guarantees such rights. The general debate was that the whole of society must do so, not explicitly the government or state, but it was not excluding the responsibility of the state. As described in the document, economic rights name a minimum of participation by all that is needed if the common good is not to be harmed.

There had been much debate at hearings, as well as among members of the committee, over the way in which work should be treated within the document. There were many who wished that we had begun the entire ethical section with the concept of work, the way in which the human person enters fully into society through work, and the way in which self-realization comes about through work. Instead of that approach, the committee dealt with work in the document under the agents of an economy and thus under the concept of worker. It was felt that this approach would help our people and make the concepts more existential and realistic.

There was also a general fear that an American audience would not look well upon such an analysis in which work becomes the central and almost determinant aspect of self-actualization. The Marxist overtones of such theories might make them immediately rejected by an American audience. Although these concepts are brought in from *Laborem exercens*, we did not begin the ethical section with that concept for the reasons just explained. There is also the tendency in American society to make too sharp a distinction between work and leisure and not see the importance of leisure in self-determination. For these reasons the section on work has not been as prominent in the document as many would wish. Perhaps that emphasis should not be taken too seriously, since it is a question more of approach and relationship of ideas than of substance.

Several times within the document the traditional concept of subsidiarity has also been dealt with. Some opponents of the document feel that this, too, should have been the central core out of which all the other concepts of Catholic social teaching in relationship to economic questions would have proceeded. The committee was not convinced that that was the proper order of thought and introduced subsidiarity as a principle, but certainly not the overriding principle, of Catholic social teaching. It has been used in its traditional sense as both a sociological and an organizational analysis. The committee also avoided the concept sometimes associated with subsidiarity that Catholic social teaching supports capitalism only insofar as it is recognized as an organization of small, independent businesses. This tendency toward making "small is beautiful" the central theme of Catholic social teaching seemed to the committee to be too restrictive and only one aspect of the whole picture. This analysis, in order to be faithful to the tradition, had to include the need for global concerns as well as global entities. Certainly Pope John XXIII recognized the need in our present world for a balance between these two phenomena.

The document thus deals with subsidiarity but also recognizes the responsibility of international and global units. Perhaps in this area (as in some other areas of Catholic social teaching, such as work) there has been indeed a slight shift in emphasis. Probably the reason for this is the need in the United States to emphasize the concept of common good and solidarity in order to balance the extreme concepts of individualism and autonomy which are so prevalent in our present U.S. society. In this the document can be seen as a very clear example of a letter to a primarily American audience. On the other hand, one must also admit that these tendencies spread everywhere throughout the world with American culture and business and are not restricted to a U.S. audience. On the other hand, it is true that a document on capitalism and Christianity produced for, let us say, a Japanese audience, may have balanced these elements in a different way.

PHILOSOPHICAL CONTEXT

One of the more interesting aspects of the Economic Pastoral Letter is the philosophical context out of which it is written. It is difficult to distinguish this context from the theological context just cited, but there are several specific philosophical issues that are at stake whenever one talks about capitalism. The predominant capitalist theories still revert back to Adam Smith and thus have a deep root in Enlightenment philosophy and liberalism. Since the history of the attitude of the Catholic Church in the United States toward liberalism is quite different than that of the Church in Europe, the philosophical questions are perhaps not as urgent as they may seem to be in other areas of the world. On the other hand, one still has to ask the very basic question about the United States culture as to its roots in Enlightenment theory and how much of that philosophical basis is still very evident in the national culture. Probably that question is being asked at this moment more clearly and precisely because of the bicentennial celebrations of the founding of the nation and of the writing of the Constitution of the United States. Many discussions surrounded such anniversary celebrations. One could say that there is in the United States right now a certain tendency to look again at those fundamental underpinnings of both the political and the economic roots of the nation.

As capitalism makes its way around the world, many of these systemic issues are indeed being discussed again, because of the contrast between new capitalist developments and the older U.S. system. These systemic questions are not asked in our letter but are often lying under the surface and appeared over and over again in hearings and symposia all over the nation.

For example, our letter does not deal at great length with the question of the profit motive. This question constantly arises in discussions in the United States today, usually under the rubric of self-interest. One could say that that basic philosophy has been extended recently beyond the question of merely economics to the political system, as well. There has been also a lengthy discussion about the *homo economicus* and how the various churches should support that kind of concept of the human person. That homo economicus is indeed often equated with an emphasis on the Protestant work ethic and on thriftiness, honesty, and those virtues that have been considered historically as synonymous with capitalism.

The larger question, however, remains: How much of the whole Enlightenment and liberal philosophy remains embedded in the U.S. culture today? One could say that it is indeed pragmatically quite strong, but theoretically quite weak. What is meant by this is that there is very little philosophical analysis of the culture and what underpins it. Nevertheless, the Economic Pastoral Letter is really the first time that the Catholic Church in the United States has faced up to the basic roots of Enlightenment philosophy that have characterized and continue to characterize American culture. The reason for this is that in the past Catholics saw themselves as a minority and did not really contribute to the public debate about political and economic issues. They accepted the freedom that was granted them in a pluralistic democratic society and fought to maintain their independence, but they did not, as Catholics, really come into any kind of open debate concerning the way faith relates to the fundamental principles of Enlightenment theory. Some readers recognized immediately that the Economic Pastoral Letter seems to be too accepting of the basic premises of liberalism and that in some respects this is a betrayal of the general tradition of the Church and its social teaching.

There is no doubt that the question of private property had to be dealt with by the Economic Pastoral Letter, and it did so in terms of the whole of Catholic social teaching from the time of Leo XIII to Pope John Paul II. One could say that the whole of Catholic social teaching has indeed been influenced by liberal thinking with regard to this question. The same could be said about the whole language of rights, and economic rights in particular, that one finds in the document. In this sense one could say that the document, like most Catholic social teaching, has indeed taken up some of the basic concepts of the Enlightenment and made them its own.

Such an approach to Enlightenment philosophy is a realistic one, although at times it is difficult to hold the extremes together. So, for example, the document accepts a kind of communitarian morality in dealing with some issues, but at the same time accepts the "rights" language and the more individualistic morality in dealing with others. One could say that one of the purposes of the document was to maintain a balance and synthesis between these two views in an attempt to bring them together rather than to take one or the other position as being diametrically opposed to each other. In this sense the document could be seen as a contribution in practice, if not in theory, to that complex issue of the relationship between equity and distribution.

It should, however, be quite clear that the document does not take the mechanistic approach to the human person and to society that has sometimes been attached to Enlightenment thinking. One does not find anywhere in the document the idea of a hidden hand or a clock theory that would give the impression that the workings of a capitalist system must be mechanistic.

That mechanistic approach is indeed rejected in favor of a modified capitalism where the human person must remain in control of the means available for assisting all and assuring the common good. In this respect the document does not seek in any manner a third way between capitalism and communism, sensing that no third way is possible within the strictures of Enlightenment philosophy, which has really produced both capitalism and communism. Instead of such a mechanistic approach, the document begins to slowly move the discussion toward other means of organizing a system that would avoid some of the pitfalls of the earlier capitalist theories. These are tentative and indeed, given the nature of the letter, must be more pragmatic than theoretical.

Thus, chapter 4 of the document, which deals with new organizational structures for the future, downplays the concepts of competitiveness and individualism in favor of concepts of collaboration and cooperation, with a greater emphasis on cooperatives and new modes of social alignment for economic development. These are only initial concepts, but the authors of the letter certainly knew that they challenge some of the basic concepts of capitalist theory and suggest new ways and new beginnings for not just practice but also for theoretical analysis. Later, in an examination of the sociological context of the letter, these concepts will be treated from a different point of view.

ECONOMIC CONTEXT

At the beginning of drafting the letter, it was evident to the bishops and their staff that the Economic Pastoral Letter was being written at a time when the science of economics was undergoing a certain change. Like so many social sciences and psychology, the aims and attempts of so many had been to conceive of economics as a kind of exact and rigorous science, like physics and chemistry. This trend toward a kind of econometrics had reached its peak before the committee began to write the document. Although it was not the intent of the writers to downgrade in any way the whole field of economics, it was thought necessary to be a bit cautious about taking sides among so many of the economists themselves concerning the nature of their science. One could say that the committee worked out of the premise that economics is indeed a science conditioned very much by human reactions and thus interrelated with psychology and sociology in ways that perhaps the more rigorous sciences do not exhibit. In fact, so many of the terms used by economics — profit motive, incentives — are more psychological than economic in nature.

Many of the former tools for analysis no longer seem to work for contemporary economics because of the global interdependency that is indeed so hard to control and to regulate. Most acknowledge that it is the end of the Keynesian period, but no new reliable theory, and with it the necessary tools, seems to pervade. When the drafting committee began the letter, there was in some sectors of the U.S. society great hopes for the supply-side theories that were more recently in vogue. It was felt by some that, by stimulating the entire economy and placing such strong emphasis on growth and productivity, most of the problems affecting the society in terms of unemployment and poverty would disappear. By the time the letter was published, much of that enthusiasm had diminished and more realistic attitudes began to appear. Poverty in the United States and unemployment had not been reduced, and there was much fear about the lack of incentives for the middle class because so many of the heavy industries that had built that middle class had been taken out of the country and gone to nations where labor was much cheaper.

There was a certain rise of enthusiasm because of the large number of new jobs in the service industries that followed, but they have not proven to be of much assistance to the general middle class, and again a period of disappointment has come in. However, probably the most difficult factor for the economist today is the analysis of the way in which the American economy interlaces with so many others, especially the Japanese and West German economies, so that analysis and predictions depend not just on measures taken in the United States but also abroad. One would have to add to this list the ever-increasing indebtedness of the nation and the effect that this has upon the inner economic stability of the nation and the world.

One could say, however, that the economic presuppositions in the pastoral letter are that it is a modified or mixed economy that is being described. It assumes that the American tradition will indeed be capitalistic and that it is important that it be humanly controlled. It has always been, the letter states, the tradition of the United States to mitigate the harsh human costs of the capitalist system by taking measures that would permit greater equity and justice. So much of the debate that surrounded the letter was on means for obtaining that kind of equity and justice, and not about the goal itself. At times some of the bishops in their public statements did feel, however, that many only gave lip service to those goals.

Some economists have felt that the economic presuppositions in the letter are already outdated and belong more to a previous generation and its war against poverty than current assumptions. Again, these criticisms have been somewhat modified in the light of the fact that the supply-side theories did not produce the results envisioned. One senses a certain realism now in looking at policies and programs that came out of the Great Society to see if one can analyze those that worked and produced good results as distinct from those that were wasteful and not helpful. The continual debate exists around welfare and the concept that welfare can create a dependency on the state and not provide the incentives needed to help people participate in society. It must be stated that there is still a judgmental approach on the part of some toward the poor and an attempt to blame them rather than help provide the skills and economic policies necessary for greater employment opportunities.

Many have criticized the letter because it does not wholeheartedly embrace capitalism as the most consonant of all economic systems with Christian belief. The bishops have pointed out that the Catholic faith does not support any economic system, but judges each one on how it affects the lives of people, especially of the poorest in society. They point out that it is not the role of the Church to approve totally any economic system, but rather to make clear from its biblical and ethical perspectives that no human system will be perfect and, therefore, that it is necessary in every system to correct those aspects that militate against human dignity and do not permit the participation of all in the good of society. It was also clear that our society had no concept of distributive justice but only of commutative justice and that many people believed the only solution was charity toward those that were poor. It will be some time before the Church is able to catechize its people to the difference between charity and justice and help them see that many of the systemic problems in the capitalist system in the United States will not be solved by charity but only by a greater awareness of distributive justice.

One would also have to say that the letter makes it clear that the political dimension of economics must also be taken into account. In a democracy such as ours, where decision making lies in elected bodies, political powers often alter and change what might be sound economic decisions for non-economic motives that go beyond the goal of pure productivity. The letter, for example, does cite in several cases the way in which the consistent military buildup in the United States and the large sums of money spent on that buildup affect the whole economy and touches the way in which money can be found and allocated to those in need. The document points out the way in which the military buildup also consumes some of the finest minds in the nation that continue to be occupied with creating ever-more-destructive instruments of war. Although there is no complete analysis in the document of the relationship between the nuclear buildup and the economic system, it is constantly talked about and alluded to. The committee did some studies on the reconversion of an economy from its present high military expenditures to a nonwartime budget concept, but did not go into great detail in the document about this approach, because it does not seem to be relevant at this particular moment.

Perhaps the most difficult aspect of the debate concerning the relationship between the document and economic theory centered around the word *freedom*. It has been used so often by economists to refer to the freedom of the person with capital to invest it and to do as he or she wishes with his or her property. In this sense, freedom is a freedom of choice open to the one who has the talent and the wherewithal in the system. The concept is not used in a univocal fashion when one compares it to the way in which freedom is used in the political arena. There is generally no attempt on the part of theorists to bring the political concept of voting and democratic choice into the economic sphere.

Our letter makes allusion to this, citing *Laborem exercens*, and does talk about this possibility of democratizing more and more the workplace. This is seen as an extension of the concept of human dignity when people have a stronger say over the decisions that affect so intrinsically their lives. The debate on this issue will indeed continue for decades to come, as it is basic to the entire set of theories upon which the capitalist system is based. The reason it seems important at this moment, however, is the gradual eroding of the middle class in the United States, where many are becoming quite wealthy while others are slipping down to the poverty edge. One senses a gap that is growing between rich and poor and a lessening of the strength of the middle class.

The question of freedom will also continue to come up because of the general decline of the power and strength of labor and the labor unions in the United States. This phenomenon has been with us for several decades now, and one could say that the labor unions have continued to lose credibility because of inner scandals and a lack of clear programs. It could also be stated that at times their demands went beyond those which were really possible for efficient business. They stand now in special difficulty because of the move of so many labor-intensive industries outside the nation. The new service sectors have not been unionized.

This critical moment in the history of the United States with regard to unions has placed the Economic Pastoral Letter in a difficult situation. The letter does not want to praise any specific union but rather to reassert the principles that Catholic social teaching has always stood for in terms of the laborer and the rights of labor. Since these are being denied so often in the United States and in the world, it seemed absolutely necessary to restate them. On the other hand, the committee did not want to be biased and ignore the difficulties that are present because of a lack of credibility of the unions themselves. They, too, have to be called to a kind of inner reform. They had been neglected by the Catholic Church in the United States for many decades since the Catholic population was no longer entirely belonging to that immigrant labor group that had been the backbone of the unions before the Second World War.

It seems quite clear, however, that the next decade will see a strong tension in the role of labor in the United States, with continued attempts on the part of industry to destroy the power that unions have acquired.

Many see in this a return to some of the struggles of the Industrial Revolution, and because of that, the principles reinstated in the Economic Pastoral Letter will be of utmost importance.

On a more theoretical plane, the question of liberty has indeed come up among economists. Many economists have analyzed the system as having very little inner liberty but as being somewhat controlled by factors outside the hands of management itself. So, for example, they often point out that the need to compete or the need to produce more profit for stockholders and owners often is so overriding that there is very little liberty for a manager to pursue policies which may seem to that manager or owner as being more humane. This question of inner freedom within the system and how much it can be controlled by human reason and effort is a theoretical question that is paramount, however, to the entire discussion.

The bishops have tried to point out the places and the way in which economic decision making intersects with moral judgments, but the question of freedom is paramount both in identifying that moment and in doing something about it. It was presupposed by the bishops that such human control is possible, even though at times it would mean taking a trade-off that from a profit point of view would not be the one most recommended. Continued discussion on this issue will undoubtedly follow and bring more light to the way in which the economic capitalist system is a morally responsible one. New discussion also will help show the limits of economics as a science and those points at which psychology, sociology, and anthropology enter in, since the system is always dealing with reactions that presuppose customs and traditions. In this respect the future will probably be an interdisciplinary one.

It should also be stated quite clearly that the document is not a complete document from an economic point of view. The bishops selected only four areas and those four areas simply do not exhaust the full gamut of an economic perspective today. So, for example, there is no treatment in the document about monetary questions, banking, and all the principles behind this important aspect of an economic system. These limitations are indeed quite evident if one reads the document and expects to find a general picture of economics and how moral decision making relates to the entire field. That lack of a complete systemic analysis is indeed a handicap, but such thoroughness probably was impossible at this moment of history. It would be hoped that various aspects would be taken up and continued, so that over a period of time a more general and complete approach could be brought forth.

SOCIOLOGICAL CONTEXT

Those who analyze the American scene are often surprised by what they seem to sense as a double standard or two value systems constantly at work in American society. I cite, for example, a passage by John F. X. Harriott from *The Tablet* in 1986:

> One seemed to be in the presence of two value-systems only tenuously connected by public relations rhetoric. So much talk of democracy, yet less real political choice than almost any European country offers. So much talk of justice, yet fearsome squalor and poverty alongside the evidences of affluence and luxury. So much talk of peace, yet such obsessions with the power of the gun. So much talk of an open society, yet a political system whose upper reaches are closed to all but the richest and dominated by vested business interests. Material standards of life which, lauded as exemplary, are yet incapable of being duplicated elsewhere without bankrupting the world's resources. Pride in the American revolution and what hostility towards any other. Pride in American democracy and justice, but deep distrust of their genuine expression abroad.[2]

As one can see from this perceptive and more recent analysis, there are indeed two divergent sets of standards that seem to pervade the U.S. climate and often are not synchronized one with the other, even though they do have the same basic roots in Enlightenment philosophy.

Often Americans are not aware of the way in which these two standards intertwine with each other. A theoretical analysis of these two sets of values or ethos can be found among current sociologists:

> Yet, despite their central importance in American life, the values of the ethos are often in conflict. Some of the conflicts arise within the same strand of the ethos — for example, the conflict between the democratic values of majority rule and minority rights. Most, however, occur between the two major strands of the ethos — between the values of capitalism on the one side and democracy on the other. In our view, the tension that exists between capitalist and democratic values is a definitive feature of American life that has helped to shape the ideological divisions of the nation's politics.[3]

One of the sources of that ethos is indeed democracy, and the other is capitalism. McClosky and Zaller have outlined the way in which these two sources are present in American society:

> However vital the roles of democracy and capitalism have been in American life, not all of the values incorporated into the ethos are mutually consistent and harmonious. Value conflicts, after all, are endemic to all complex societies, including the United States. Among the most important of these, as we have suggested, are the conflicts that arise from the differing perspectives of the two traditions. Cap-

italism is primarily concerned with maximizing private profit, while democracy aims at maximizing freedom, equality, and the public good. From this difference, others follow. Capitalism tends to value each individual according to the scarcity of his talents and his contribution to production; democracy attributes unique but roughly equivalent value to all people. Capitalism stresses the need for a reward system that encourages the most talented and industrious individuals to earn and amass as much wealth as possible; democracy tries to ensure that all people, even those who lack outstanding talents and initiative, can at least gain a decent livelihood. Capitalism holds that the free market is not only the most efficient but also the fairest mechanism for distributing goods and services; democracy upholds the rights of popular majorities to override market mechanisms when necessary to alleviate social and economic distress.[4]

These conflicting signals, if you will, are often not evident to Americans themselves but constitute a kind of American "civil religion" that is frequently analyzed by current sociologists. It often makes it difficult for countries to whom the United States relates to understand exactly what is happening and which ethos is operative at the time. Often third-world nations seem to feel that the capitalist ethos is operating in dealing with them and the democratic ethos becomes somehow neglected. One could say that in the last decade there has been a strong emphasis on the values that spring from the capitalist tradition in the United States, with a certain downplaying of the exportation of its democratic ethos.

So often in the past it was the democratic ethos that tempered some of the less human aspects of the capitalist ethos and was the source of "moral sentiment," about which Adam Smith spoke, that was so needed as a hidden hand to bring about more equity within the society. A closer analysis of the two sets of values and how they operate in the United States would indeed help our general picture of the Economic Pastoral Letter. One could, however, say that the letter is an attempt to strenghthen the democratic ethos at this moment of history and to provide support for a tradition which has helped to mitigate the human costs of a rapidly expanding economy.

There is another kind of dichotomy in the United States which is also a part of American civil religion and provides a clear sociological background to the letter and also a clear background for the pastoral plan that must accompany a letter of this sort. The bishops of the United States were not naive about the difficulties that will be encountered in trying to implement this document and make it truly a document of the Catholic population and those who support a similar value system. It has become more and more clear in the United States now that the individualism upon which so much of this nation has been founded becomes indeed one of the deterrents toward a more operative and a more realizable concept of the common good. The hyper-individualism in American culture has been reinforced recently with so much pop psychology and has become almost synonymous with a generation that sociologists called the "me" generation.

The book that has analyzed this tension most clearly is *Habits of the Heart: Individualism and Commitment in American Life*, by Robert N. Bellah, Richard Madsen, William M. Sullivan, Ann Swidler, and Stephen M. Tipton. That recent study says the following about American culture:

> The tension between self-reliant competitive enterprise and a sense of public solidarity espoused by civic republicans has been the most important unresolved problem in American history. Americans have sought in the ideal of community a shared trust to anchor and complete the desire for a free and fulfilled self. This quest finds its public analogue in the desire to integrate economic pursuits and interrelationships in an encompassing fabric of national institutional life. American culture has long been marked by acute ambivalence about the meshing of self-reliance and community, and the nation's history shows a similar ambivalence over the question of how to combine individual autonomy and the interrelationships of a complex modern economy.[5]

It must be clearly stated that the hyper-individualism that the capitalist system spawns permeates all aspects of life in the United States and makes it difficult to establish a communitarian ethos. There have been many attempts at this throughout the history of the United States, and these attempts have almost always ended in failure. The fact, however, that they remain a constant experiment is indeed indicative of a kind of natural need on the part of Americans to balance their hyper-individualism with a sense of community and with a need for greater support from within the community. (A recent study of these attempts in the history of the United States can be found in *The Simple Life: Plain Living and High Thinking in American Culture*, by David E. Shi, New York: Oxford University Press, 1985.)

According to modern analysis, this hyper-individualism has affected very much the stability of family and many other social institutions. These have also had effects upon the economic stability of the nation. On the other hand, one could not deny that the development of the talents of each individual has indeed contributed much to the development of the entire society. Thus the document makes no negative comments in theory about the entrance of so many women into the workforce of the United States. This has been seen as a contribution to their own development and to the nation. Nevertheless, it was necessary in the document to point out the inherent difficulties in this movement and the risks to the stability of family that are being taken by it. There is a certain tendency in the letter, however, to try to strengthen the community sense and solidarity and thus to balance the hyper-individualism that is so rampant. That attempt will require much pastoral programming on the part of the bishops and one can only expect a certain modicum of success within the near future.

One of the other aspects of the American scene which has affected the sociological milieu in which the letter is being promulgated is the attitude on the part of Americans toward government. There is no doubt that there has been from the very beginning of the nation a negative attitude on the part of many toward government or the state in general. This attitude was a part of the founding groups because of their search for freedom from restraints in Europe and oppressive governments. It is also inherent in much capitalist thinking, in which the government plays almost no part or, at most, a regulatory role that would stimulate competitiveness. This concept has been taken to extremes in some instances where a libertarian philosophy that would almost reduce government to nothing can be found. There are, however, certain inconsistencies, because many libertarians who espouse almost no government in economic issues espouse at the same time very strong and powerful government in terms of military buildup.

Habits of the Heart talks about that ambivalence toward government in the American population:

> In our interviews, it became clear that for most of those with whom we spoke, the touchstones of truth and goodness lie in individual experience and intimate relationships. Both the social situations of middleclass life and the vocabularies of everyday language predispose toward private sources of meaning. We also found a widespread and strong identification with the United States as a national community. Yet, though the nation was viewed as good, "government" and "politics" often had negative connotations. Americans, it would seem, are genuinely ambivalent about public life, and this ambivalence makes it difficult to address the problems confronting us as a whole.[6]

Because of this general negative attitude toward government, many viewed our document as statist, that is, every time the bishops mention that the government should be a part of the solution for a social problem, it angered a certain group of Americans whose general philosophy leans toward ever-less government.

The Economic Pastoral Letter is, however, positive toward the role of government, although indeed it does envision a limited role. It follows the general division of society into three groups: the state, the private economic sector, and mediating structures such as labor unions and churches. It does not see the role of the state as going beyond its own prescribed limited domain. Nevertheless, there has been a tension in the U.S. population over the way in which the role of the state is presented in the Economic Pastoral Letter, depending on how much the individual has or has not accepted the minimal role of government that has been a consistent part of the American tradition. For this reason, it was very difficult for us to discuss words such as "economic planning" in the letter. This immediately scared many readers, because it enters into the domain of the role of the state. Although one could talk at great length about the need for all to be involved in planning and not just the state, nevertheless, the spectre of a totalitarian state planning system has always been present there.

There is no doubt that the American population at this moment needs a more positive and optimistic attitude toward government and a clearer view of its role in the economic development of the nation. This becomes ever more evident when the government must deal with other governments in terms of any kind of international economic inequity. At that moment there is no one but government to assume the leadership role. These ambivalent feelings will indeed affect the attitudes that many have toward the pastoral implications of the Economic Pastoral Letter.

WORLD CONTEXT

Although the document itself does not begin with a complete analysis of global interdependency, nevertheless that concept is constantly in mind throughout the entire document. In general one could say, however, that the American population is not yet totally aware of that context in which its economic future is taking place. The implications of a global economy and of being interdependent in that economy have yet to strike most Americans. Our letter presupposes this global aspect and tries to extend to the rest of the world the principles applied to the U.S. economy concerning human dignity, participation, and the option for the poor. We state in our document the need for a different kind of education in order to take one's place in that kind of a new world.

In preparing the letter, there was also a broader consultation outside the United States than for any previous document ever produced by the U.S. bishops. On the other hand, one can sense that this is but the beginning of a process that must include a constant dialogue between the Church in the United States and the Church in developing nations. It would be hoped that the beginnings laid down by this document will not be lost in subsequent years.

The document also insinuates that greater dialogue is necessary between the United States and its consistent allies and partners in the capitalist project. There is much to be learned from the way in which capitalism has developed in newer nations, as well as the renewal of capitalist thinking in Europe. These aspects have not been dealt with adequately in the letter, although they are constantly on the minds of those who read it. Such a global perspective will indeed continue to permeate the thinking of those who deal in any way with moral issues and economic questions. It is hoped that the letter lays the basis for such future dialogue, because that is indeed its intention.

The letter also laid the basis for a broader ecumenical dialogue than has previously been known for any document in the United States. One could say without exaggeration that the ecumenical input into the Economic Pastoral Letter has been the greatest of any document coming from the Catholic Church. The Jewish community in particular has resonated well with the biblical section dealing with the Hebrew scriptures and has been most cooperative in formulating that section as well as the principles that flowed from it and the practical consequences for our society. It has been helpful also in strengthening the concept of solidarity and common good.

The Protestant Churches have been working on similar projects and contributed their information and analysis to the committee. It would be hoped that their projects and the one of the Roman Catholic bishops could be the subject of continued dialogue. They are strong in their biblical analysis but often then leap to immediate application without a sense of the philosophical implications and how those are to be integrated into the entire ethical theory. One could say, however, that almost all mainstream Protestant Churches in the United States have been dealing with this same subject and have already produced small but worthwhile reflections on the same issues being thought out by the Roman Catholic bishops.

CONCLUSIONS

The writing of the Economic Pastoral Letter was an endeavor that took much time and effort on the part of the American bishops. On the other hand, they felt a duty to face up to the fact that the American economic system has a strong influence on the morals of the nation and therefore was indeed an apt subject for their reflection in the light of the gospel. They know also that it was necessary to bring to the present moment of history the lights of the tradition of Catholic social teaching and its biblical heritage. They know the imperfections of their attempt as it begins to relate to the policies that should affect the nation.

In making this study they also know that they are but beginning a very long and difficult process that will involve two aspects of their lives. First of all, they will have to reflect more and more about the way in which these principles affect the inner life of the Church as an economic actor. They know that this will be a great challenge to the Church in the United States in terms of the way in which the Church treats its own employees and the way in which the rights of employees are safeguarded. Especially since Vatican Council II, there has been a larger and larger number of lay people hired by the Church. This has been partly because of the great expansion of the Church in the United States, but also because of the loss of a number of religious, especially women religious, who comprised the greater part of the Church's workforce in the United States. Those women worked so zealously and were paid so little. Now it is necessary to hire lay people for almost all of those positions, and the question of salaries and benefits comes immediately to the fore. It will also be necessary for the Church to examine its properties and investments and the way in which it functions within that capitalist context.

Most of all, the Church realizes that it will be challenged to bring the gospel message to the life-style of itself and its people. This challenge will mean a stronger sense of the role of liturgy in creating a sense of community, one that is indeed more than just a natural community but one that has a supernatural end. There is no doubt that the document is quite aware of the role of the Church as one of going beyond that of merely altering human structures and systems. It points out very much the need for a larger perspective in analyzing the role for Church. On the other hand, it does not deny that the Kingdom as preached from the gospel will indeed affect structures as well as the consciences of individuals here and now at this moment of history.

It also realizes that it must begin a very slow pastoral plan so that the hope outlined in the letter can become a part of the vision of its people. Some of the obstacles have already been outlined, and these will have to be continually dealt with in the decades that follow. Indeed the bishops know that they are only at the beginning of a large project but feel that the guidance of the Spirit and the collaboration and cooperation of the entire Church will bring them to a better realization of their tasks and their obligations as moral leaders in a nation as large and influential as the United States at this moment of history.

CHAPTER 11

The Economic Pastoral Letter Revisited

Since the time of Pope Leo XIII, Catholic social teaching has become an integral part of the Church's self-consciousness.[1] The body of that teaching has grown most rapidly in recent years for two reasons. First, the document of Vatican Council II on *The Church in the Modern World* has brought social issues more clearly into the light of the gospel and its practical application to our times. Secondly, many nations have taken up the challenge of Pope Paul VI in *Populorum progressio* to make an analysis of the applications of the teaching necessary to an ever-changing situation in every nation. In doing so, new problems have been faced and new plateaus reached.

The Economic Pastoral Letter of the bishops of the U.S.A., *Economic Justice for All: Catholic Social Teaching and the U.S. Economy*, passed overwhelmingly by the U.S.A. bishops in November 1986, is perhaps the most extensive of these national reflections. By now the immediate impact of the document has ceased, and it is time to assess some of its strengths and weaknesses in the light of a constantly changing economic scene. In fact, one could easily say that the document would not be written in the same way if it were written today. Changing times demand a fresh look. In this article I would like to examine just a few of the areas that were not treated at great length or were treated inadequately in that pastoral letter—items that may be of more importance for the future.

SYSTEMIC CONSIDERATIONS

As the eastern bloc moves from its Marxist approach to economic issues to a more capitalistic stance, many questions about the very systemic nature of capitalism arise. These were being asked earlier but were avoided in the bishops' letter, lest it turn out to be an academic treatise rather than a pastoral document. It is inevitable that a comparison must be made today between the U.S. approach to capitalism, which is deeply rooted in Enlightenment philosophy, and the present practice of such countries as Japan and Korea, which have not known an Enlightenment in their history and have a different mix of private and public sectors as well as a different societal makeup that is less individualistic. Many are posing again questions about the very nature of capitalism and what happens to it in a culture that has sprung from a different philosophical matrix.

The Economic Pastoral Letter avoided an in-depth analysis of these questions. It was agreed upon at the outset by the writing committee that the approach would not be theoretical but rather phenomenological.

The short paragraphs in the letter that treat of the systemic questions are found in the middle of the document, almost buried there, and seldom cited (par. 128–131). Here the bishops try to be evenhanded, but in reality accept that the system as such is not immoral, and then proceed to point out ways in which it must be improved. The debate over the essentially immoral nature of capitalism that has raged for decades in Latin America was avoided. On the other hand, all know that it has not been solved to the satisfaction of most participants.

Since the publication of the first draft of the Economic Pastoral Letter in 1984, the contributions to this debate in the theological sphere have not been numerous. It should not be surprising that most of this type of discussion has taken place outside the U.S.A. I would like to cite here two noteworthy contributions.

In November of 1985, Cardinal Ratzinger gave a talk in Rome to a group of assembled German industrialists. His talk was entitled "Market Economy and Ethics."[2] The cardinal framed his remarks around four sets of questions. Given his general theological positions, which are so contrary to the whole Enlightenment project, it was not surprising that he raised some of the most critical questions about the free market and its philosophical roots.

His first set of questions emphasized the contradiction between the claims of freedom and the deterministic nature of the market system. "Deterministic in its core (*in ihrem eigentlichen Kern deterministisch*)," was his description. Thus, he stated, the system can, but does not necessarily, work for the common good. The development of the spiritual powers of the human person must also be a part of the economic agenda, and here the capitalist system has nothing to contribute. He sums up these first observations saying that the "market rules function only when a moral consensus exists and sustains them."

In his second set of questions, Ratzinger brings forth the inability of the market to help those nations where the inequality is so large that they find themselves outside the competitive arena and thus seek centralized economic controls as the only answer for themselves. Although these attempts have not borne the fruit some may have hoped for, the author does not a priori dismiss them as morally unfounded.

Thirdly, the cardinal questions the ability of the Marxist approach to solve the question of inequality, since it too is deterministic, more radically so than even liberalism. Here he sees points in common in the deeper philosophical presuppositions of the two systems. One would expect that the cardinal would reject this Marxist approach because of its reduction of ethics to history and party strategy.

The fourth set of questions the author raises in terms of a dialogue between Church and economy are those that the bishops of the U.S.A. totally avoided. In their crassest form they are summed up in a quote from Theodore Roosevelt, made in 1912, that Cardinal Ratzinger cites: "I believe that the assimilation of the Latin-American countries to the United States will be long and difficult as long as these countries remain Catholic." He also quotes a 1969 lecture of Nelson Rockefeller in Rome, where he recommended replacing Catholics in Latin America with other Christians, an undertaking, Ratzinger asserts, that is in full swing. It is not surprising that Ratzinger recalls the thesis of Max Weber that certain Christian denominations have a closer affinity to the capitalist agenda than others.

Ratzinger shows a certain negativism with regard to post-World War II economic development and the role of the U.S.A. He said in that lecture in 1985: "On the other hand, we can no longer regard so naively the liberal capitalistic system (even with all the corrections it has since received) as the salvation of the world. We are no longer in the Kennedy-era, with the Peace Corps optimism; the Third World's questions about the system may be partial, but they are not groundless." Here the cardinal opened up the old controversies about capitalism being more congenial to some denominations than to others, an argument that most have intentionally avoided in past decades, at least since the writings of Max Weber on the Presbyterians and capitalism. Should it be opened again? The cardinal certainly thinks so.

These ambiguous statements by the cardinal, not taken to their ultimate conclusions, show a deep distrust of the capitalist system, especially as manifested in the U.S.A. By phrasing his concerns more in the realm of questions, he does not have to find an alternative solution. He comes the closest to doing this when he states that the subjective and the objective in ethics in the economic system must meet, specifically in those handling the system itself. "It is becoming an increasingly obvious fact of economic history," he remarks, "that the development of economic systems which concentrate on the common good depends on a determined ethical system, which in turn can be born and sustained only by strong religious convictions."

Ratzinger does not openly condemn capitalism as intrinsically evil, but he does come close to it in the many questions he raises. Perhaps this is why his lecture, given to a conservative group of capitalist industrialists, has not been much quoted by the neoconservative economists or political writers. He makes the point quite clearly that the former discussions on this point are not finished. It is disappointing that Ratzinger does not go further into the area of objective ethics, as he called it, in the economic realm. It would have led him into the kind of systemic analysis that is needed from an ethical point of view. Nevertheless, his conference raises some of the most serious objections to capitalism and its determinism that can be found in Catholic literature today. Theologians of liberation theology might be surprised by his defense of their criticisms of capitalism.

But the most extensive and comprehensive critique of the Economic Pastoral Letter of the U.S.A. bishops comes from Brazil, from the pens of Clodovis and Leonardo Boff. Writing in the *Revista Eclesiastica Brasileira* in 1987, these two authors make a lengthy and minute examination of the Economic Pastoral Letter under the title, *"A Igreja perante a economia nos EUA – Un olhar a partir da periferia."*[3] I omit here the words of praise that are raised about the letter to get at the substance of the most severe criticisms they launch against it. The tone of the response is clear and friendly, even when it is basically critical.

They object to the fact that the capitalist system itself was not called into question. "Without doubt the American bishops strike vigorously at the apparatus; yet, they do so only to repair it and not to replace it." The reason they sense the American bishops are not capable of tackling the system as such is that the basic presuppositions of their socioanalytic tools do not permit them to do so. One could say that the basic difference here is that the two authors do not perceive of any middle class in their analysis of society. They see only the rich and the poor, even when they approach the American phenomenon. They are correct when they state that in the U.S.A. the option for the poor is not an adversarial slogan that pits one group or class against another. Class conflict is not the type of analysis used by the American bishops and this, in the mind of the Brazilian authors, vitiates the analysis used.

Perhaps, however, a deeper division in approach is evident in that the American bishops did not accept the economic dependency theories that make the poverty of the third world the result of exploitation on the part of the capitalists of our first world. This causal relationship is nowhere accepted in the Economic Pastoral Letter of the U.S. bishops, but is presupposed by many Latin American authors.[4]

It must be asserted that these theories were examined by the bishops' committee drafting the letter, but never accepted as proven. Other elements, such as corruption in Latin American governments, had to be factored into the equation, as well as the enormous amount of capital flight taking place from Latin America to the U.S.A. Nevertheless, the lack of clear analysis of the position that the American bishops were taking on these points, so crucial to Latin American authors, diminished the enthusiasm with which the letter was read and accepted by other areas of the world.

The two strongest criticisms from this sector thus are focused on the fact that the bishops did not have a clear and enunciated social theory to accompany their economic analysis, nor did they answer the question raised by Latin Americans based on the dependency theories: Is poverty, or is it not, an integral component of the capitalist system? Is the capitalist system intrinsically evil? Does it exploit the poor to fill the coffers of the rich?

Thus they criticize the letter as being a functional analysis of capitalism, not a systemic one. They do not believe that the system can be repaired and fixed, because it is systemically flawed. They also criticize the letter as taking only an ethical and never a political approach to economic issues. That is why such words as *exploitation* or *domination* do not exist in the letter, they say. This criticism joins that of some other critics in the U.S.A. who found the letter totally lacking in a perception of the relationship between economics and political power.

For all these reasons the authors find the document of the U.S.A. bishops flawed, even though they praise its worthwhile attempt and openness.

These two approaches to the systemic questions, that of Cardinal Ratzinger and that of the Boff brothers, that were for the most part omitted in the Economic Pastoral Letter, are cited because they do point out an agenda that is not finished. Because the American bishops did approach the subject in a functional manner and not in a theoretical and systemic way, they have left themselves open to criticism that the basic philosophical foundation from the Enlightenment upon which capitalism and free-market economies are based has not been carefully scrutinized for its ethical content. This task remains as yet undone.

There seems to be a need to do so today, not just because of the third-world analysis and experience, but because of the new kinds of approaches to capitalism from Japan, Korea, and now the eastern bloc. How much of the Enlightenment roots are left in those new phenomena?

Another reason for pursuing this examination comes from the large number of scandals in the U.S. economy in the last decade that are of much concern, namely the Wall Street abuses and the pathetic and tragic situation of the savings and loans. Not to examine how these may be indigenous in the system because of greed and the tendency to monopolize would be a lack of objective research. It seems that we can never get away from the whole theory of greed and when good self-interest turns into pernicious greed. Does the system make such distinctions between the subjective and the objective almost impossible?

ETHICAL VERSUS BIBLICAL CATEGORIES

The drafting committee of the bishops made the decision that the presentation of principles that should be used to judge an economic system would proceed on two parallel tracks. The first would be a biblical analysis, the second would be ethical, in the sense that it would come out of the Catholic tradition of using the natural law and more philosophical approach. It was hoped that in this way the debate in the public forum could take place on specifically Christian grounds, that is, from the biblical perspective, and then also from the philosophical point of view to engage those who did not share our biblically grounded faith.

Probably this approach mirrors the state of moral theology in the Catholic Church today. Nevertheless, it was soon seen in the discussion that followed the issuing of the Pastoral Letter that this sharp distinction was not necessary. There was a need to bring these two approaches together into a single synthesis. Most readers who shared our values but not their biblical basis did not see a need to separate the two categories. Most Catholics would have liked to have seen the two joined; they wanted to see the philosophical supported by the biblical vision.

This project of joining the two visions is a necessary one. Such a composite vision would gain more support for the convictions that derive mostly from natural-law theories. Perhaps the area where the joining of the two would be most difficult is the whole question of subsidiarity. To my knowledge there has not been a moralist who has shown how that concept, as proposed by Pope Pius XI and used by every subsequent Pope, fits into a biblical perspective. Even its derivation from natural law is not clear. It is just stated as a fact or a principle by Pope Pius XI and not rationally based in scripture or in any traditional philosophical system. Its historical roots are evident from what it is fighting against, namely, state corporatism, but its source in Catholic tradition is not clear.

This question has a certain importance, since it serves as a link to so many other Catholic approaches to society, government, and economics. Does it inevitably lead to the principle that small is beautiful? Even in its original formulation and in the way it has been repeated by papal documents, it admits that some issues are of such a nature that they can only be decided by the larger national or international bodies.

Many of the questions and some of the terminology of the classical writers on capitalism should also be examined in the light of the biblical vision. For example, the question of self-interest and its excess in greed has not been analyzed carefully. I am not sure that the terminology is good. Perhaps one should rephrase the whole issue, today in particular, not in the light of greed or self-interest, but in the light of the obligation, personal and communal, to take care of one's responsibilities. Even the accumulation of wealth, not just its creation, must be seen in such a light. There should be a way of seeing the creation of wealth as having as its first purpose the common good and, as its second aim, that of helping the individual take care of personal and communal responsibilities.

The fear exists that these issues will continue to haunt the discussion if they are not faced squarely and correctly. The Economic Pastoral Letter of the U.S.A. bishops treats economic questions in a positive way: It tries to see how the system should function, what aims it should have, who should be affected by it, and how all should participate in it. These are all admirable aims. But the letter does not treat of the dark side, the dangers and pitfalls, so explicitly. These questions are not analyzed as minutely as the goals that should be there because they have traditionally been seen as more in the realm of private morality. But the issue remains of how private or subjective morality affects the whole question of the functioning of the system itself.

Perhaps this is the perspective that Cardinal Ratzinger raises when he says that the objective and the subjective aspects of the ethical discourse in economics should be joined. Greed is a subjective aspect that influences the running of the system. Exploitation of workers is a subjective ethical question that affects the outcome of the system. One could name many more of these subjective issues. Their biblical roots should be evident.

The objective questions, on the other hand, deal with the whole issue of the built-in qualities of the system itself, which tend to cause the system to malfunction or function in a way that is harmful to society or the individuals in it. For example, monopolies have always plagued capitalism. Since the system is based on competition, monopolies endanger the system. From this perception arose the need for clear governmental regulations so that competition, being essential to the system, can function in a way that benefits all and respects the rights of all. The Economic Pastoral Letter does not treat explicitly of the whole question of monopolies and how in the history of the capitalist system, if some outside regulatory force is not present, monopolies prevent the system from working for the good of all. This systemic question is most important today, when there is no international force that can regulate monopolies in an economy that is already international and interdependent. Perhaps no other systemic question will be so urgent for capitalism in the future than that of monopolies.

Questions about chronic recessions and the resultant unemployment are systemic issues. The whole area of inequities and the manner in which the rich seem to get richer while the poor seem to have so little access to the capital needed to enter the system is another systemic problem. This problem is more talked about today than even when the Economic Pastoral Letter was issued. Such inequalities in society, where the gap between rich and poor continues to grow at such a rapid pace, is a systemic issue, since it derives from the way the system functions. The "haves" have more to invest and their wealth grows at a faster rate. Taxing was usually seen as one of the principal ways of equalizing such growing gaps, but taxing is outside the system and acts as a corrective to the system itself.

For capitalism, government has become the great regulator. But the role of government can also be positive in stimulating the economy, in providing funds for research, and the like. This role of government is crucial to any analysis of economic theories and practice. It is not clear in the Economic Pastoral Letter how government and the economic factors intersect. In the hearings, we heard both from those on the more libertarian side of the scale, who held that least government is best and that the market would regulate itself and those who were inclined to socialistic solutions that involved government at all levels. These issues that center around the role of government and the economy are still unsolved, but they are of extreme importance if one looks at the new scene today. The rising capitalist nations have a different perspective on the relationship between the state and the private sector than the U.S.A. In this respect our history is unique.

The Church in its social teaching has had a positive attitude toward government, more positive than that of many current political groups in the U.S.A., but it has not tried to ground that view—taken, for the most part, from natural-law tradition—into its biblical vision.

In this same area of concern, many rightly criticized the Economic Pastoral Letter as naive, in that it did not treat of the relationship between power and the accumulation of wealth. The Latin American critics used the categories of money and politics quite freely in their critique. There is no doubt that this lacuna does pose a problem in the letter. Perhaps it would have entailed a keener analysis of the role of economic entities in the U.S.A. and their influence on the political system. I am sure the bishops thought this would have taken them far afield from the original intent of the letter. On the other hand, one cannot omit the fact that there is a close relationship between government and the power that comes from money and its use. The Bible has much to say about this latter question, but to my knowledge no one has asked similar questions concerning power and its proper use in biblical terms.

These questions become ever more real to us as we see the power of international financial entities in comparison to the financial, political, and social power of many nations. Some businesses are more powerful than the nations they function in.

In this connection, the discussion of economic power enters into the whole question of the role of nations, the rights of nations, the sovereignty of nations. Since our economy is now international and interdependent in its scope, and since the boundaries of nations in this regard have become less clear, the whole question of the concept of nation is now being brought into question. This issue will grow as one of the most important in our contemporary history. We see so many areas of Africa, Asia, and especially now the eastern bloc, assert their historical national roots, based as they are on racial and ethnic diversities, at a time when, economically speaking, the question of nations is posed in a serious way with regard to viability in the future.

The Economic Pastoral Letter seemed to ignore these larger questions, even though it was aware of the need to confront the new economic situation that is one of interconnectedness around the globe. Questions of government and its role, questions of monopolies in an interdependent economy that defy national boundaries, the effects of monopolies on economically weaker nations, questions of national sovereignty in the light of multinational corporations that are bigger and more powerful than the nation itself—these issues go beyond the biblical and ethical vision that is presented in the letter and demand a new look in a new world.

In this respect one could also say that the environmental issues were not faced in the letter. The section on agriculture in the original plan was to treat of natural resources in general. The drafting committee had already proceeded to hearings, for example, on coal and like resources. All of this issue involved the future of this planet as such. This plan was not followed because of the urgency of the farm situation, but that does not mean that the issues of natural resources and ecology were unimportant for an analysis of economic structures and will disappear. They must also be treated from the biblical perspective.

BIBLICAL SPIRITUALITY AND THE ECONOMY

Although many commented favorably on the final chapter of the Economic Pastoral Letter as being practical and helpful, there was still some feeling that it was not helpful enough. It was not clear to priests how to preach the abundance of material found in the document. It was also not clear to many of the laity how to apply these principles in their daily lives and in the workplace. They appreciated the role of liturgy and the fact that the Church itself must be just in its economic relationships, but they wished more of a blueprint for themselves.

Perhaps the most difficult pastoral task that is yet to be accomplished is to make people aware of the communal nature of their vocation both as a human person and as a baptized member of the Church. This is a question of attitudes that must be faced if the contents of the letter are to be put into practice. So many sociologists point out the nature of our society and the Lockean individualism that permeates it. These fundamental influences, which go way back to the founding of this nation, have been recently reinforced by psychological concerns about the self that can reach the point of a kind of collective narcissism. Combating such extreme individualism but coupling it with a wholesome respect for self and one's identity and worth will not be easy. The best way to help the economy, however, is to alter some of the selfish attitudes that pervade the society. In this way the goals of society change and the aims of the economic system are broadened.

Simultaneously, people must become more aware of their societal duties. We have used frequently the phrase "common good" in Catholic social teaching in the past, but it is not an active concept in the lives of so many. The Church's approach to economic issues is very much connected with this term. Other modes of expression, such as solidarity and participation, are helpful and useful.

Perhaps the most difficult attitude is one of moving from charity to advocacy. Charity is a necessary Christian virtue, but it is not an economic solution to any problem. It is easy to preach charity and thus alleviate the signs of a problem at once. But the ultimate solution must be to help people participate in the life of society by making their contribution and not becoming wards of society. To this day I cannot understand those who criticized the Economic Pastoral Letter as being a proponent of a large welfare state. This distorts the very message of the letter, which was one of participation. In the opening paragraphs that was made clear as one of the marks upon which an economic system would be judged.

Nevertheless, people do need more help in sorting out in their daily lives how they should respond to the economic system that is ours.

They also want to know how they should live in a society that is market driven and where they are bombarded daily by so much advertising and forced to consider so many things they do not need or want. These perennial questions are now joined with those of ecological concern on both a micro and macro level.

Such problems of living a good Christian life in this day and age are compounded by the international, intercultural, and interracial aspect of our world. We now relate also to those who live thousands of miles away from us. Here the contrasts of rich and poor are even more startling and seem even more hopeless.

Perhaps one of the principal duties of the Church today should be to continue to give everyone a sense of his or her individual worth, while at the same time trying to create for all the incentives that are needed to take care of one's own responsibilities and then to contribute to society. The Church did well in the past in this area, and there is every reason to feel that it can continue to do so now.

Catholic social teaching, and in particular the Economic Pastoral Letter of the U.S.A. bishops, is not an economic plan for the future, but the values in them are indeed valid for building a better and more just future for all on the planet. The times we live in are constantly asking for new reflections on how we can and should build a more equitable future for all. The values are not outmoded, even when the practical solutions demanded seem to change with the times. Catholic social teaching gives a vision of the human person who functions in an economic society according to his or her intrinsic worth. It does not neglect that the aim and destiny of the person goes beyond this earth, so all economic systems will have their deficiencies and human limitations.

The next decades will be crucial for this planet and for the welfare and human dignity of each person who lives on it. These same decades will pose a special challenge for Catholic social teaching. It is only at the beginning of its important reflections begun one hundred years ago by Leo XIII.

PART IV

AFTERTHOUGHTS

CHAPTER 12

Signs of the Spirit
in Our Age

Both within the Church and in society today, people ask more than anything else for signs of hope.[1] If there is one single question repeatedly posed to me within the Church, and most especially by priests, it is: How do you keep up your own hope? It seems that people find, in this last decade of the century, so few signs of hope in the world and even in their own Church. Our generation has seen in the dissolution of the Soviet Communist empire what one would almost have to call a miracle. That does not seem to have been enough. In fact, for some it aggravates the situation, since they see no one, no group, that is taking advantage of the new moment to bring to the world a sense of purpose, a direction where everyone can feel that they are a part of the decisions that will affect their existence. They do not see their Church as a leader in this post-Communist world.

Most often it is those who were expecting unprecedented changes in the Church after Vatican Council II and then in the world after the demise of Communism who now seem to see few signs of lasting hope. Time is, as it were, running out and nothing is happening. On the contrary, they see their Church as turning in on itself, as becoming more and more closed to the world, as ever more restrictive and small-minded.

In addition, almost everyone sees in the world itself so many overpoweringly negative signs. How often we read about the sad state of our world. These pessimistic indices that are lifted up include the drug culture, the breakup of the family and social structures, the many ethnic wars, the senseless murders both in our inner cities and in our rich suburbs, the oppressive poverty that one finds juxtaposed with extravagant riches, the cult of violence, and so on. There is no end to the litany. Every preacher knows how easy it is to start with such a jeremiad in order to bring people to their knees. The list does not have to be elaborated. We have all experienced these evils in one way or another.

But there are also signs of the living Spirit among us. We know that God

141

loves us now no less than God loved previous generations of believers. When I am in need of hope and must see signs of the Spirit working among us, I read the Acts of the Apostles. There one sees the vivid evidence of the life of the Spirit working among the early believers. When one remembers that it was with simple, for the most part, uneducated people that Christ started his Church, it brings consolation and encouragement. We must remember that the Kingdom belongs to God and that God has more at stake in bringing about the Kingdom than we do. We must then marvel that God chose to bring about the fullness of that Kingdom with such fallible instruments, such broken vessels, as us humans.

Frequently one hears the expression "the signs of the times." Most often it is used by Catholic writers to mean signs of the Spirit working in our day. At other times it seems to mean just general tendencies in society and the world, without any value judgment on whether or not such trends are under the guidance of the Spirit. I prefer to use the phrase "signs of the Spirit" to avoid such confusion, this indicating that the movement in question is positive and that in it we must discern the action of the Spirit. Borrowing a phrase from the Book of Revelation, we must ask what the Spirit is saying to the churches now, in our own time. These signs are not always clear and unequivocal and thus one must constantly discern the appropiate response. They are most often opportunities, what the Greeks called a *kairos*. Seeking the right response is something best done in dialogue with others who share a similar quest. That is why ecumenism and the newer forms of dialogue and discernment in the Church are so important.

When Pope John XXIII first used the expression "signs of the times" in his encyclical *Pacem in terris,* he used it in this positive way. Vatican Council II followed by using the same kind of terminology. What is important in the phrases "signs of the times" or "signs of the Spirit" is the theology that underlies such expressions and thinking. It is the belief, above all else, that the Holy Spirit is found in the whole Church and thus, through baptism, in all its members, not just in one segment of it. In addition, the action of that Spirit cannot be contained by us within the confines of our own or any particular Church. The Spirit is not to be put into a straitjacket or restricted to our own plans and programs. The Holy Spirit operates at will, out there ahead of us in history, pulling us on, forcing us into new thinking, opening up new vistas. The Spirit is active in the world and we must discern in that action a vitality that is more expansive and less limited than our own. It is the Spirit who is the true builder of the Kingdom that Jesus Christ announced and brought into being here among us. On our part, it means an openness to the light of the Spirit, a readiness to respond. It means we must not be defensive or closed to the changes the Spirit might demand of us. It also makes all of our plans in Church and society provisional, subject, that is, to the need to discern what God wants of us and where the Spirit is leading us. Even in our own works of justice and love we are never alone; they must be responses, too, to the work of the Spirit.

God's Spirit is seen as the indispensable "Other," the first and most important partner in all our actions and plans.

BECOMING CATHOLIC

One of the signs of the Spirit in our day is the trend toward finally becoming catholic or universal, not just in name but also in fact. This trend is found, first of all, in the secular world, but it brings about a new perspective in the Church as well. One of the concrete realities of our moment in history is that we are in every way becoming a global civilization. Economically, as a nation, we are no longer able to be independent of other nations. Such interdependency is not always felt equally by all nations, but the fact remains that what happens in one corner of the globe is immediately known by all, affecting every other part. We are bonded one with another in ways that have never been known in previous history.

I have mentioned the insight of Karl Rahner that, since Vatican Council II, we are now entering for the first time in the history of the Church a phase where all races, all cultures, all nations are not only represented but must be full and participating members. For that reason, we can say that we are becoming catholic. We are no longer a Church of western civilization; we are an African, an Asian, an American, as well as a European church. But we Catholics are not ready for such pluralism, nor are we being prepared for it. In fact, the opposite is occurring. The tendency to over-centralization that characterizes the Roman administrative offices in our Church today is a knee-jerk reaction to such pluralism, a tendency to try to control it in every respect lest it get out of hand. The major issues of our day will be to discern how we can retain that cultural pluralism, how each culture can embody valid expressions of the faith, how these various expressions can enrich and sustain one another, and, still, how we can keep the bonds of unity in faith and charity that are so important among disciples of Christ.

Unity in diversity will be the constant tension of our times, in society, but also, and perhaps more so, in every aspect of Church life. The limits of pluralism will be constantly tested, as is already evident in the inner life of our Church today. Theologically pluralism poses many questions that we must face squarely. There is no single unifying and accepted philosophy that underpins our theological thinking, as was true in past centuries. There is no single cultural matrix that helps bind us all together; there is no Roman Empire, no overarching canopy of western civilization. Because of the fact of pluralism we must constantly be asking what the non-negotiables in our faith really are, what the hierarchy of truths might be. In the past we often fought battles over what now seem to be useless issues. (In the Benedictine Order we would say that some in the Order would go to war over a *quilisma* or an *ictus*.) In the new global history of our Church we must be clear as to what is really important and what is not. Such a distinction demands discernment, detachment, and humility. We must also remember that points that seem unessential to theologians or even bishops can be very important to people in the pew. Unfortunately, there is a tendency to rush toward an external unity through catechetical formulae and not see the need for faith to be embodied in cultural expressions and in the life and holiness of the believers.

Such a quest for unity does not mean that everything unessential is discarded or unimportant. Often these items can be important to one's spiritual life and growth, but they should not be imposed on the whole or made the touchstone of orthodoxy.

Here in the United States we have an unprecedented chance to experience and reflect on such pluralism because we find it also within our borders as a nation. By reason of history we are a microcosm of the world situation. In so many ways the Catholic Church in the U.S.A. is also a microcosm of the universal or catholic community of believers. We are blessed here with much cultural diversity because of the immigration movements, not only of the past, but most especially of the present. The recent ones, especially the Hispanic newcomers, have been slower to accept the melting-pot theory and have kept the experience of cultural pluralism alive for us. Reflecting on our experience can be of help to the universal Church—even at the times when some might not want to hear what we have to say. I do not believe in that kind of "American Messianism" that can so easily be nothing but pride and presumption, namely, the concept that the U.S.A. is some kind of chosen instrument of the Kingdom and thus favored by God. But I do believe that there are certain advantages that one nation or section of the world has at a given moment of history to further the understanding of the gospel and the Kingdom. The Church in the U.S.A. today has so many of these advantages given it by history.

There is a concern among so many Catholics in the U.S.A. that we are not playing our full role in the discussions within the universal Church about the future, that the whole thrust is toward Europe, especially Eastern Europe, Africa, and Asia. We are not seen as intellectually serious people with something to contribute. Instead, we are often looked upon as naive, spoiled, pragmatic, and frivolous. At the deepest level of Church life, we are, thus, expected to receive orders, not to be a part of discerning and studying, of dialoguing and contributing. Nevertheless, because of the unique position that the United States has in today's world, our cultural values and disvalues—whether one likes them or dislikes them, approves of them or disapproves of them—are the dominating forces as the world culture begins to emerge. For example, it is our jeans and our music that have captivated the global culture. If one turns on the TV anywhere, in any country, one will see reruns of the common soap serials that were made here in the United States or local imitations of them. To ignore that strong and pervasive U.S. culture would be disastrous for Church and world.

But there is more to it than jeans and soaps. We are also experiencing as Church the integration of a new scientific mentality and new psychological perceptions into our religious vision. Receiving new attitudes is not a new phenomenon for the Church, but what is new is to see this experienced on a global scale. Just as one saw the philosophical basis of neoplatonism integrated into theology by Augustine in his day, or the writings of the Arabic philosophers brought into Catholic theology in the high Middle Ages by Aquinas, so we will now have to reflect on all the new findings of science and psychology in the light of faith for our day. This integration must also be done at a moment when there is no longer a common philosophical language, as in the past, and when there is also a new thrust toward a less precise and even more pluralistic biblical discourse. In sum, not only must we deal now with a cultural pluralism but also with a new pluralism of knowledge, one which poses new challenges to us as a catholic and global Church.

When I feel at times a bit discouraged at the lack of visible progress in such an integration and the lack of thinkers such as Augustine or Aquinas, or when I see the unwillingness on the part of so many in authority to permit such rethinking, or when I see the reluctance on the part of many to accept that such an integration is even needed, I recall the early centuries of the Church. The Golden Age of the Church in the fourth and fifth centuries was also the time of the most numerous heresies and schisms. Vitality and diversity often bring with them such unwanted but seemingly inevitable scars. It is much better to have such debates about religious values than to find that religious issues are irrelevant or unimportant. The fact that they are so often discussed and debated in the public forum is a sign that religion is vital to the human enterprise at this moment of cultural upheaval. That in itself to me is positive. There are many who, until recently, were predicting the opposite, namely, that by our day, as a result of a continual secularization process, religion would be relegated to insignificance and held on to by only a few less intelligent people. That prediction has proven false.

The Spirit is calling us to be catholic, global, multicultural, and to embrace all human knowledge of self and society, of the universe and its limits and capabilities. To me this call is indeed a sign of hope.

SHARED RESPONSIBILITY

In *Pacem in terris* Pope John XXIII mentioned as one of the signs of the times the thrust on the part of the working class to take control of their destiny. This move toward democracy has seen its fulfillment in our day with the fall of the Eastern bloc. Everywhere in the world we see people claiming the right of self-determination and the freedom that it entails. One should not be surprised, then, if the same trend is found within the Church. The contrast between the society we live in and the structures of the Church makes this trend even more pronounced. People find it difficult to live a kind of schizophrenic existence, responding constantly to two different kinds of structures. Moreover, they are not totally convinced that the present Church structures must remain forever as they now are.

The response most often given by the hierarchy is that the Church was not set up by Christ as a democracy. But our people also know that neither was it set up as a monarchy or a dictatorship. The keys were indeed given to Peter according to Matthew, and to all the apostles according to John, but both Gospels stress that the style of authority must also be different from that exercised in the world, as Christ himself made evident on so many occasions. An authority of service, an authority that is also under the yoke of the gospel, is indeed a different kind of authority.

The makeup of the Church is unique and includes many aspects that present a contrast with secular democracies. By baptism everyone is equally incorporated into Christ, receives the Holy Spirit, and becomes a child of God. Through that baptism one becomes a full and integrated member of the Church. Because of that membership in the body of Christ, through baptism, every member shares also in the mission of the Church. That mission is the same as the mission of Jesus Christ—the salvation of all peoples—and is not just the prerogative of the leaders. All receive the fullness of the Holy Spirit. God can speak and act through the lowliest in the social or Church structure.

One notes in the Acts of the Apostles how everyone in the primitive Church was a part of the decision-making processes; the whole community was involved and seemed to give their approval to the major decisions, even those of a dogmatic nature. There is, thus, a legitimate tradition that goes beyond that of making of the faithful silent spectators in the functioning of the Church. This appreciation for the role and authority of all the faithful did not simply emerge in our day or as a product of the Enlightenment; one finds it throughout the history of the Church. We see it clearly in the Acts of the Apostles where the whole community was of one accord in the solutions proposed to theological issues. In history it is seen just as noticeably in the election of the hierarchy itself. Bishops were often elected by the acclamation of the faithful and this model is still reflected in the election of the pope. To this day the pope is elected by the college of cardinals in their capacity as pastors of the major churches of Rome. For that reason each cardinal, with his nomination, is also named to a titular church, a parish of the diocese of Rome. One should, thus, not so easily say that the Holy Spirit cannot make heads or tails out of democratic processes or that more democratic ways of determining an election or a course of action are totally outside of the Catholic tradition.

But there is more to the issue. Because the Holy Spirit is given equally to all in baptism and since all share in the responsibility of the mission of the Church, there has been a tradition in the Church to consult that living Spirit. In the *Constitution on the Church* of Vatican Council II (*Lumen gentium*) this is explicitly described in the following terms:

The holy people of God has a share, too, in the prophetic role of Christ when it renders him a living witness, especially through a life of faith and charity, and when it offers to God a sacrifice of praise, the tribute of lips that honor his name (see Heb. 13:15). The universal body of the faithful who have received the anointing of the holy one (see John 2:20, 27), cannot be mistaken in belief. It displays this particular quality through a supernatural sense of the faith in the whole people (*supernaturali sensu fidei totius populi*) when "from the bishops to the last of the faithful laity" (St. Augustine, *Predestination of Saints* 14, 27) it expresses the consent of all in matters of faith and morals.[2]

This passage, taken almost verbatim from the writings of John Henry Newman, describes what has become known as the *sensus fidelium*.[3] As Newman outlines the tradition in his works, one sees that the unqualified statement that the Catholic Church has never known anything like a democratic principle, even in matters of faith, is not totally true to history. I leave aside here the whole theology of reception that is much discussed in our day after the encyclical *Humanae vitae*. These aspects of the tradition may not be entirely worked out yet but that does not deny that such currents of thought existed and continue to exist in the Church.

The legitimate fear of many is that the Church could, without serious reflection, accept the democratic processes of our culture and attempt to apply them in a way that would do us harm. That fear is real because we are not *tout court* a congregationalist church; we do not hold that the Holy Spirit is found in 51% of those voting at any given moment of history. Often God speaks to us through the silent whisper. God cannot be so bound by our categories. It is God's Kingdom and not ours. That plan must be discerned in faithfulness to the past and with courage for the future. Moreover, our tradition is that of being a hierarchical Church. We accept the passages in Matthew and John seriously about the keys and the power they confer. But the hierarchy, too, must see the Kingdom as belonging to God, and recognize as well the need to discern God's plan in history and not impose their own personal one. Scripture and tradition are normative for the whole Church, including pope and all members of the hierarchy. Working out these various prophetic roles, as they are called by Vatican Council II, is not easy. It should produce, however, a model unto itself that has democratic aspects as it has had in the past and that recognizes the life of the Spirit in all members of the Church.

Some today, I am not sure how many, would like to ignore these subtleties and simply be told what to believe, even in those areas which are not essential. So often they also simplistically reduce the teaching authority of the Church to papal magisterium alone and seem to make no distinctions among various papal statements, whether they are encyclicals, homilies, or just remarks at public audiences. Even interviews given by the Prefect of the Congregation for the Doctrine of the Faith become infallible in their eyes! That kind of solution will not endure, even though some in the hierarchy might like it or find it easier in some respects to deal with. However, the reduction of the teaching mission to the pope alone, the leveling of all teaching to a category of infallibility, the lack of a distinction among the various kinds of papal pronouncements and statements, the quasi-infallible quality given to the official and unofficial statements of the Congregation for the Doctrine of the Faith—all of these tendencies are not in accord with our tradition.

The problem we face with shared responsibility is that the very size of the Church is and will be against us. For a global Church to find structures and means that will permit shared responsibility on all levels while respecting the genuine role of the pope and bishops will not be easy. But, in light of the legitimate desire of all the faithful to assume their proper role in the mission of the Church, it is very important that we try to find these structures and means. To deny this rightful development in the Church will cause many wounds that will fester into the future. We must recapture our early roots that saw the Holy Spirit in all the people of the Church and thus the need to listen to that Spirit as it speaks through the Church. I might recall in this regard the idea of Pope Paul VI that among the electors of the pope should be included the members of the Council of the General Secretariat for the synod of bishops. He floated this idea in a speech to the Roman curia in 1973. Needless to say, the curia squelched that suggestion rather rapidly. The advantage this suggestion holds is that bishops and not just cardinals would form the electing body which would thus represent a broader spectrum of divergent views. It also would avoid the undemocratic procedure that seems to scandalize many in our modern world, namely, that the pope appoints as cardinals those who agree very naturally with his own way of thinking and he thus guarantees that his successor will be of the same mold as himself. There is some, but less, chance of that happening if members of the synod were to be a part of those electing the successor.

Another misperception that must be avoided is to think of the laity in the Church today as uninformed or bewildered sheep. That laity is often better instructed than the pastors, and more zealous as well. They are not so easily scandalized as some would assume. If they are scandalized, it is more often by unjust or unfair procedures than by theological error. We do a disservice to our lay people if we do not see them as mature, committed, intelligent, discerning adults.

In our tradition, supported by theological distinctions, there are different manifestations or paradigms of shared responsibility. This diversity must be respected, even though it is often misunderstood and there is a tendency to equalize everything.

Collegiality is the first form of shared responsibility. The word is often used to mean any kind of collaborative ministry, but it should be restricted to the relationship between the bishops and the pope and the relationship among the bishops themselves. At ordination a bishop becomes a member of the college of bishops, hence the word collegiality, and shares with the pope the governance of the universal Church. Vatican Council II makes that clear and unequivocal. Chapter 3 of the *Constitution on the Church* (*Lumen gentium*) outlines the teaching on the role of bishops in moving terms. It never permits the reader, however, to lose sight of the fact that the bishops must be constantly united to the pope and never can act outside that unity. These words sum up that teaching:

> For the Roman pontiff has, by virtue of his office as vicar of Christ and shepherd of the whole church, full, supreme, and universal power over the church, a power he is always able to exercise freely. However, the order of bishops, which succeeds the college of apostles in teaching authority and pastoral government, and indeed in which the apostolic body continues to exist without interruption, is also the subject of supreme and full power over the universal church, provided it remains united with its head, the Roman pontiff, and never without its head; and the power can be exercised only with the consent of the Roman pontiff. ... This college, in so far as it is composed of many, expresses the variety and the universality of the people of God, but in so far as it is gathered under one head it expresses the unity of the flock of Christ.[4]

On the other hand, the council has some striking words to say about the role of the bishop in his own diocese. Phrases that Catholics had been used to hearing only about the pope are now used for the bishop. Note the following:

> The bishops govern the churches entrusted to them as vicars and legates of Christ, by counsel, persuasion and example and indeed also by authority and sacred power which they make use of only to build up their flock in truth and holiness, remembering that the greater must become as the younger and the leader as one who serves (see Luke 22:26-27). This power which they exercise personally in the name of Christ is proper, ordinary and immediate, although its exercise is ultimately controlled by the supreme authority of the church and can be circumscribed within certain limits for the good of the church or the faithful.[5]

This paragraph makes clear that the image of the relationship between the pope and the bishops is not similar to that of a main or central office in relationship to the branch offices as found in any business corporation. It emphasizes that the bishop's role and power are a part of the office itself and not delegated to him by the pope.

This theory is clear and traditionally sound. What is needed in our day is a working model of how it should all function. Perhaps the reason for this tension is that certain roles within the principle of collegiality are not fully explained nor examined. So, for example, one could ask what is the role of the Roman curia or even the Apostolic nuncios with regard to this collegiality. Are the bishops who work in these offices equal partners with the bishops of the world, or do they somehow stand above them? If they are but extensions of the papal ministry, making that office more functional and effective, then why are they made cardinals, archbishops, and bishops? Do these orders just obfuscate their relationships to other bishops in the college of bishops and thus cause confusion? Sometimes these Roman offices put out documents on their own accord, sometimes saying that the pope has ordered them to put out the document in question. What is the effective collegial role with regard to such documents? What kind of consultation among the bishops of the world is needed or at least useful before the issuing of such documents?

I could go on and on asking such questions about the practical functioning of collegiality and the role of the Roman curia. But one would also have to ask what the role of the cardinals is in this collegial body. From a sacramental point of view they are but bishops; there is no mention of them, thus, in the documents of Vatican Council II as having some very special role to play with regard to the whole question of collegiality. From that purely theological point of view they are but bishops like all the others and should then function simply as other bishops. But in reality that is not true. Their particular prestige means that they are, in the minds of the faithful and in practice, somehow superior to the other bishops. Moreover, they are also often used to form a special council by the pope, to be consulted on very specific issues of a sensitive nature. Thus, they become in this way a kind of collegial body within a collegial body, even though there is no theological basis for this role. Theoretically and for the sake of consistency they should be consulted, as the pastors of the diocese of Rome, on those matters that affect that particular local church. However, they no longer function that way except when they elect a new bishop for that see, who is then also pope.

Perhaps the most important innovation since the council has been the emphasis put on the national conferences of bishops. They are to be expressions of the kind of collegiality outlined by the Vatican Council but as exercised among the bishops of a geographic region. Their advantage is clear and they have been, for the most part, very effective since the council. Much theological discussion still persists over their teaching authority but from a pragmatic point of view they have been effective instruments of pastoral coordination and, in a restricted way, also of governance in the local churches. It seems that they are undergoing special tensions at this moment. Their relationship to the Roman curia is not clear. Unfortunately, there is the fear that undue interference in the actions of the local conferences on the part of the curia is making both effective and affective collegiality more difficult. Some bishops seem to be more favored by the curia or are put into the role of seeming to push the curia's point of view, an attitude that breaks the affective nature of collegiality and can cause distrust.

Perhaps one of the most difficult questions to be worked out with regard to collegiality as it is now expressed and exercised is that it could, if abused, militate against the rise of any kind of effective leadership among the bishops. If the appearance is given that all must think alike and act alike in the name of collegiality, then no prophetic voices can rise up among the bishops. It becomes then, in the name of harmony and unity, a seductive way of silencing voices that might sing a different tune. Collegiality does not mean that no debate is possible or that all must enter a discussion with the same ideas; such a position would be ridiculous. It must permit differences of opinion and honest free discussion if it is to be an effective instrument of collaboration among bishops and between the bishops of the world and the pope.

Is the relationship between a bishop and the priests of the diocese to be modeled on that of the relationship between the pope and the bishops? The answer it seems to me is no. By ordination a priest shares in the ministry of the bishop and becomes a member of the presbyterate. This is expressed liturgically by the imposition of hands by all the priests present. They do not ordain but show through that gesture that they are accepting the new priest into their body. Vatican Council II makes it clear that "the bishop's office of service was delegated to priests in a subordinate capacity."[6] They are spoken of as collaborators with the episcopal order. Because of that act of being joined to the episcopal order, they share in the authority "with which Christ himself constitutes, sanctifies, and rules his body."

Hence the priesthood of the presbyteral order presupposes the sacraments of Christian initiation, but is conferred by the particular sacrament in which priests are sealed with a special mark by the anointing of the Holy Spirit, and thus are patterned to the priesthood of Christ, so that they may be able to act in the person of Christ, the head of the body.[7]

It is not my intention here to restate all that the council says about priesthood and its role in the building up of the body of Christ. My interest is on the question of how the priest exercises his special shared responsibility. That question is outlined by the Council in these words:

All priests share with bishops in one and the same priesthood and ministry of Christ, but in such a way that the very unity of their consecration and mission requires their hierarchical communion with the order of bishops; this they fittingly express by concelebrating from time to time in the liturgy, and by proclaiming that it is in union with them that they celebrate the eucharistic meal. In view, then, of the gift of the Spirit given to priests in ordination, bishops regard them as necessary helpers and advisers in the ministry and office of teaching, sanctifying and shepherding the people of God. ... [Bishops] must be very ready to listen to them, indeed to ask their advice and to discuss with them all that concerns the pastoral needs and well-being of the diocese. To bring this about there should be set up, in a way appropriate to modern circumstances and needs, a council or senate of priests, with a constitution and rules to be determined by law, to represent the priests of the diocese and to give effective help to the bishops, by their advice, in the running of it. ... Close union between priests and bishops is needed all the more today in that, for a variety of reasons, it is necessary for apostolic initiatives not only to take on many different forms, but to go beyond the limits of any one parish or diocese. So no priest can adequately fulfill his charge by himself or in isolation, but only by combining his efforts with those of other priests, under the leadership of those who preside over the church.[8]

The document goes on to say that by ordination the priest joins the presbyteral order which forms one body of service in the diocese attached to the bishop. The image is one of a single priestly ministry, namely that of Jesus Christ, shared by the priests through their union with the bishop.

Some of the same questions asked earlier about the relationship between the bishops and the Roman curia could be asked about the relationship between bishop and priests. In saying that priests are like extensions of the bishop it could give the impression that they are but puppets, automatons, and that again no prophetic voice can arise. It would be unfortunate if that image dominates. The correct image is that of the single pastoral service of Jesus Christ that all share in being effective in one portion of the globe through mutual insights and supports that bind bishop and priests. I would prefer to see it as a group of mountain climbers roped together and mutually concerned about each other. Or perhaps a more homey image would be better, like that of a main chef, cooks, and waiters at a banquet, making sure that the needs of all the faithful are being satisfied.

The model of shared responsibility here is more functional, more locally restricted, more personal in a very certain way because of the smaller numbers that permit a greater capability for sharing. The pastoral needs of these people in this geographic area are discerned together by bishop and priests.

But what is the role of the laity in these models of shared responsibility?

One could answer that their input must be present on all levels but according to the characteristics of each level. On the parish level it is now taking on a clearer image. The experience that we are gaining with parish councils has helped to define that role more effectively. There still remain problems of clarification of powers and of roles, of leadership functions and of administrative details, but in general there has been progress. Perhaps one of the major problems has been that lack of continuity on the part of so many members of such bodies and the lack of a real understanding of the specific nature of "consultation" in Church practice. Such consultation is absolutely necessary; it provides the possibility of listening to the Spirit. But it is not a part of our democratic processes and thus must be learned by Catholics. We are not used to the discipline needed to listen to what the Spirit is saying through all the people of the Church.

One should also remember that the relationship between the priest and the laity in his parish is not the same as that between pope and bishops, on the one hand, or between the bishop and his priests, on the other. It is unique. The laity have their right to participate in the mission of the Church by reason of baptism. It is not a shared ministry delegated by the priest or the bishop to them.

On the diocesan level there have been some gains but much has yet to be done. Where it is a priority of the bishop, the diocesan council functions well; where it is relegated to a secondary level, it is not of much help. The two councils indicated in the new Code of Canon Law—the Pastoral Council and the Priest Council—can be effective instruments of shared responsibility and most helpful for discerning the needs of the faithful.

On the national and international level there seems to be no effective means yet of lay participation. Some conferences of bishops have tried to work out a lay council at that level, but without great success. In the United States there is a lay advisory committee that goes over the agenda of the bishops' meetings and comments on the items to be presented. Their opinion is listened to but one cannot say that there is a real and lively dialogue between the laity and the bishops about that agenda. The priests seem to be left out at that level of discussion. On the universal level no form has emerged. At synods of bishops in Rome laity are often present and permitted to speak but they are not representative. Instead they are carefully chosen, represent only one point of view, and seldom engage the bishops in any kind of dialogue or debate.

One can only wonder what the future will hold in this respect. Perhaps the enormous dimensions of the task of listening to all make it seem impossible, but one must never stop dreaming about creative possibilities if one is to be true to the signs of the times. One has to think of the advantages of such sharing on a global level and how such contacts could enrich the Church and most especially all its individual members. What has to be remembered here is that all of these new processes and hopes are under the action of the Spirit and correspond to the new moment in which the Church finds itself, as it raises up the dignity of the baptized everywhere on the globe and sees the people of God as truly possessing the fullness of the Spirit.

A NEW SPIRITUALITY

One of the signs of the Spirit in our day is the new spirituality that has arisen. Much of this gain has been due to the liturgical renewal that followed Vatican Council II. Perhaps the most significant change was the proclamation of the biblical readings in English. That innovation and the insistence that the priest preach on the biblical text has caused a renewal of interest in the Bible among Catholics. For the first time in centuries Catholics are beginning to study the sacred texts and become acquainted with them—a practice formerly associated only with Protestants. It is true that at times some Catholics fall into a fundamentalistic interpretation of the Scriptures, one that is not consonant with our tradition, but their number is small.

At the same time we have been blessed to have a whole school of sound biblical scholars who have helped our people understand the Bible. In this way most have been able to avoid the pitfalls of fundamentalism. One could say that we are again returning to being a biblical people.

But our spirituality has also become more liturgical. People want and demand a good liturgical experience. Formerly they went to Mass on Sunday out of an obligation imposed by the Church under pain of serious sin. Now they go because they sense the need for such spiritual nourishment in order to be true followers of Christ. They find a new unity in the Eucharist. They feel encouraged and strengthened in their task of bringing Christ to the world where they live and work. Thus, they search for the parish where they can find that kind of good liturgy. This is a positive sign and also an encouraging one.

In addition to the new spirituality that is both biblical and liturgical, one could say that, for the most part, it is also psychologically sound. We live in a very psychological culture here in the United States and thus must integrate that part of our daily way of thinking into our spirituality. As one reads the great mystics of the Church, one is surprised how psychological their writings are. Since spirituality also deals with human experiences, they are the subject of human analysis too. If it is good psychology, it will be good spirituality. If something is bad psychologically, then one should rightfully question its spiritual benefits.

There is some concern because of some of the psychologically unsound phenomena that one finds in the Church nowadays. The increasing number of new apparitions and visions leaves one wondering. These are usually not a good sign in society and in the Church. One could say the same thing about a preoccupation with manifestations of the devil. It would be a loss if a sense of the presence of evil and of the evil spirit in the world were lost or even diminished. Nevertheless, history has shown that a constant preoccupation with the forces of evil leads to a distorted and psychologically unsound spirituality. The story of the resurrection is one of triumph over

Satan and those forces of evil. Not to believe in that triumph in our world today is not to believe in the victory of the resurrection.

There has also been a return to some devotional and religious practices in the past years that is to be commended. Many of these are wholesome and their return points to a need for more intimate spiritual practices for our people. The introduction of a solid devotional practice with regard to the Blessed Virgin is much needed. One sees so much that is not wholesome in that regard, so often bordering on the superstitious or what could be called spiritual "extortion," one, namely, that threatens disasters if some act is not performed. It is rare that the Church, so rapid in attacking abuses that seem to be theologically too progressive, corrects these aberrations from good theology in Marian devotion, because they seem to have a more conservative veneer. In this area of private devotions one should truly be able to pick and chose what is helpful to the individual, although some are more traditional and have held up under the test of time. It is admirable to see a return of devotion to the Blessed Sacrament.

The charismatic renewal has also enriched the Church in our day and brought a new awareness of the action of the Spirit among us. When it avoids elitism, when it shies away from putting emphasis solely on external or emotional phenomena, when it does not become too attached to fundamentalist and extremely narrow theological and biblical positions, and when it functions within a good ecclesial framework, it can be and has been a solid benefit to the whole Church.

The desire for retreats is also a sign that people are seeking deeper spiritual renewal in their lives. The retreat movement has not waned. Sometimes it is accompanied by other movements, such as the Cursillo, and that too can be wholesome. In all these movements one senses a need to belong to a larger group but at the same time to grow personally in one's faith and in one's relationship to Christ. One should also not neglect to mention the trends toward developing the contemplative dimension of our tradition as found in the movement toward centering prayer and the like. These signs of the renewal of the mystical and contemplative dimension of the Church's tradition are signs of the Spirit in our day.

In this desire for spiritual renewal on the part of so many of our laity one finds a reason for hope. It is a new and good challenge to our priests who must respond to that desire of the laity by a deeper holiness and search on their own part. Clearly, the Spirit is very active in our day.

ECUMENISM

Ecumenism is one of the truly important signs of the action of the Spirit in our times. Some may feel that this movement has fallen on hard times, but it is irreversible. When the history of our age is written, the ecumenical movement will be high on the list of those responses to the Spirit that made a difference. It might not be too clear where it will all end and there are reasons for frustration, but the striving for Christian unity and for closer bonding among the great religions of the world will not cease.

On the Catholic side it seems that the ecumenical movement has come to a halt or at least has reached a plateau. Many fears have arisen, especially those that touch Catholic identity here in the United States. One should not be surprised at these fears. For over a century we identified ourselves over against the Protestants. We saw this nation as a Protestant one and felt like outsiders. It is not easy for us now to see what we have in common with the Reform movement.

There is also the fear that some of the erosion in numbers has been the result of the ecumenical movement, a kind of spirit that says that it does not matter what church one belongs to since all churches are alike. We are accustomed to seeing Protestants change from one denomination to another and thus fear this will become the pattern for Catholics in the future.

At times we sense that there is a fear of theological relativism: "It does not matter what one believes, as long as one is okay with God." Americans tend to downplay speculative or theoretical issues and become immediately practical; thus it does not matter what one believes, some would say, as long as one acts correctly.

These fears are subtle and not too often expressed. One hears them more frequently among the more conservative branch of the Catholic Church, people who were a bit fearful about the whole Vatican II enterprise. They seem to be saying now, "I told you so." How seriously these fears should be taken is not clear. Personally I feel they are exaggerated and that the overwhelming majority of Catholics are happy and proud of their ecumenical advances since Vatican Council II.

The positive results of the ecumenical movement are even more evident than the negative ones. The fact that Catholics see what they have in common with Protestants is a gain. The result is that both have begun to define themselves over against secularism and not in relationship to each other. In fact, we are proud that we have gained and contributed to the life of our partners. On the receiving aspect we can say that we have profited much from the Protestant experience in our search for our biblical roots. We have long admired their preaching from the sacred text and have begun to imitate that tradition. On the other side, we know that we have contributed to their knowledge and understanding of the sacraments, of the three-fold ministry of orders, namely, deacons, priests, and bishops, and to a keener sense of the whole role of service and ministry in the Church.

Ecumenism has also helped all of us make some necessary distinctions. We are forced to explain the weight of our convictions, the certitude of our teachings, the sources of our doctrine, the historical searchings and winding paths. It is not that we want a least-common-denominator religion, but just that we must be more exact in explaining what we really believe and where our sources can be found. It is not a question of pick-and-choose religion, but one of how much weight and certitude we bring to the table.

Ecumenism has also forced us to avoid empty slogans and rigid positions on both the right and the left that have more to do with advocacy for a cause than a common search. We avoid the kind of purism that does not permit dialogue and that breaks unity by its very attitude of superiority and omniscience. We avoid also that kind of isolationism that does not permit growth. More than anything else, ecumenism has taught us so often to look behind controversy to causes that may not always be theological nor matters of faith. We prize unity now more than ever. Any temptation to new divisions of any sort are easily squelched. We all know too clearly the price that one pays for such disunity.

Lastly, ecumenism has permitted us to be involved in many shared projects that are examples of common discipleship. Working for a more just world is not a matter of mere expediency but comes out of sharing the same biblical vision and hope. The numerous projects that must be the objects of our gospel witness point out that we must never give up the ecumenical dimension of our present lives. That united public voice will grow stronger as the years progress.

When one has worked for a long time in ecumenism, one sees that it is also a way of proclaiming the gospel. Disunity is a sign that the message is not credible; working toward unity presents the gospel as a message of love and reconciliation. The gospel is proclaimed each time we work visibly for unity. St. John in his description of the Last Supper shows Jesus saying just that. Working toward unity is a sign of the unity between Christ and his Father and makes his message more believable. Unity, he tells us, leads to belief.

If there is any present movement that is under the guidance of the Spirit, it is the ecumenical one. We are privileged to live in this age where all sense that need for unity.

CHURCH AND WORLD

When Marx said that religion was the opium of the people, he meant that it tended to deaden their desire for a better life as they waited for the next. Their seeming neglect of this world could be blamed on the Church's teaching that one should just wait for one's reward in the next life. The Church never really taught that kind of a doctrine without qualification. Nevertheless one would have to admit that the Church had not worked out a clear relationship between this world and the next. It must now reflect on the new circumstances of the world and how it will relate to a society in which it no longer aspires to be the state religion. A sign of the life of the Spirit among us is the belief that this world counts and that somehow what happens here and now will be a part of the Kingdom as it is brought to fulfillment by the Spirit. Sometimes this is expressed by newer concepts; some, for example, see the human person as a kind of co-creator with God in bringing about the Kingdom. I personally shy away from such exalted terms, as they seem to lean toward a kind of neo-pelaganism, but the basic concept still remains clear: the Kingdom of God is brought about in the here and now. This world counts because it is the *locus* of the Kingdom coming into being.

Pope John Paul's way of saying this will surely become the classic reference for the future. He mentions that the social dimension of the gospel does two things; first, it "points out the direct consequences of that message in the life of society," and secondly, it "situates daily work and struggles for justice in the context of bearing witness to Christ the Saviour."[9] This simply says what Christ had preached, namely, that we cannot separate love of God from love of neighbor; we cannot separate saving our souls from how we live in society; we cannot separate sacraments from life.

The essays in this book are permeated with that teaching and are the source of its inspiration. At the same time, we have seen that there can be no social gospel that is divorced from the liturgy and from the prayerful reflection on scripture. Social action is never a substitute for prayer. Common worship and prayer are not only the inspiration for the works of justice but nourish them and form the common bond that keeps all believers working together for the common good. The social dimension of the gospel becomes another aspect of discipleship and makes what one does relevant to the whole divine project.

This new attitude toward the world forms the basis of all lay spirituality and has been an enrichment for the lives of so many. I sense that it is one of the most important works of the Spirit in our age.

THE ROLE OF WOMEN

Pope John XXIII in *Pacem in terris* spoke of the new role of women in society, how they were becoming ever more conscious of their human dignity, how they would not tolerate being treated as inanimate objects or mere instruments, "but claim, both in domestic life and in public life, the rights and duties that befit a human person."[10] One could add that women are seeking these same rights within the Church. I see this as being a part of the workings of the Spirit in our age. This new perception means that the Church will have to rethink its position on women, the historically accepted one, namely, that women are the weaker sex, fickle, incapable of self-determination, and so on. That concept, which postulated a basic inferiority, did not always dominate in practice and, thanks be to God, the history of the Church is full of examples of outstanding women leaders. Pope John XXIII saw this movement toward equal dignity on the part of women as the result of true Christian teaching. He noted with pride that it is especially in Christian nations where this new awareness has arisen.

We have not yet fathomed what this insight will mean for the future. My fear is that we will wait too long before taking it seriously, thus alienating more and more women. The Church's voice in society is muted by its inability to integrate women totally into its own life. Its preaching of the gospel will remain wounded until it solves this essential question for its future. Women of wisdom, the *pars sanior*, not the shrill voices on both extremes, will have to articulate this new vision for us so the dialogue will be fruitful and productive. I see only suffering ahead for the near future and hope that out of such purification a new and deeper vision will arise.

The heart of the question lies in the role of women in ministry and the question of the ordination of women. It is not clear how we can extricate ourselves from the theological knot with which we find ourselves bound. I believe most experts will say that the position of the Congregation for the Doctrine of the Faith in *Inter insigniores* is very carefully worded, does not talk about an intrinsic metaphysical impossibility but simply states that the Church does not see itself as having the power to change this tradition that goes back to its origins. The supportive arguments, most experts say, are not apodictic proofs but arguments *ex convenientia*, i.e. of fittingness, and are found in the realm of the fullness of sign and symbol. The Vatican document is clear in this regard:

Having recalled the church's norm and the basis thereof, it seems useful and opportune to illustrate this norm by showing the profound fittingness that theological reflection discovers between the proper nature of the sacrament of order, with its specific reference to the mystery of Christ, and the fact that only men have been called to receive priestly ordination. It is not a question here of bringing forward a demonstrative argument, but of clarifying this teaching by the analogy of faith.[11]

Many, in a most unconvincing way, have tried to take these arguments, such as the *symbolic* nature of the relationship between Christ and the Church, namely, that Christ is the spouse of the Church, and apply them in a *metaphysical* way to show that a woman cannot fulfill that role. Symbols cannot be turned into metaphysics. To do so in this case could lead, by the same logic, to the illogical assertion that only women, since they in this symbol represent the feminine component, that is, the Church, can be members of the Church. These arguments cannot be metaphysical ones but must remain on the level of symbol and the fullness of symbol.

It is not my purpose to argue the issue in question, but to point out the consequences. We are in an unsatisfactory position. There seems to be no light at the end of the tunnel.

And yet, I am convinced that this movement toward the rights of women and the acknowledgment of their human dignity in both world and Church is under the action of the Spirit. Where it will lead is not at this moment clear.

VOWED LIFE

To the list of workings of the Spirit in our day in Church and society, I want to add that of religious life. It may seem strange to consider something that many would judge to be in decline as a sign of the Spirit, but I feel that religious life has not seen its demise, as some may think. I have only to look around to see the large number of religious who have been faithful to their commitments and have blossomed into full and vital disciples of Christ to say that there is still much life and vitality in that form of following Christ.

If all Christian life is a dying and rising, then the example of religious, especially women religious after Vatican Council II, has been remarkable. They were the first to take that Council seriously and to put it into practice. It is true that many saw that they could just as easily contribute to the mission of the Church in the world without remaining in vowed life, but the questioning and renewed searching that followed in the religious congregations has not been in vain. The results of the general chapters show this new spirit.

One should also note the new forms of temporary experiences in religious life that follow from new modes of adhering to the charisms of the congregations. I refer here to all the lay volunteer groups that have risen up. They are numerous and fill a needed gap. They are almost a new form of religious life itself, temporary but nonetheless genuine.

The Church will always need the prophetic and charismatic elements that are represented in religious life. It would be a dull and imbalanced Church that did not have their presence. They challenge and bring the Church to new dimensions by their radical adherence to the gospel and to the following of Christ without reserve. One has always said they keep the eschatological dimension of the Church alive and before the eyes of the faithful. That could be seen as a kind of abstract and uninviting vocation, but, in reality, they simply emphasize those qualities of discipleship that could so easily get lost in the busyness of our world. Total concentration on the gospel ideal will always be needed in our midst.

Of all recent divisions in the Church and in Church law, I regret that between religious life and secular institutes. It has never seemed to me to be based on good theology, especially after Vatican Council II and its teaching on the relationship between Church and world, nor on the lived experience of so many. Almost all religious groups have been a hybrid, not neglecting the world but moving it to a more Christian dimension. I wonder if the desire to clarify and divide has not done harm to the action of the Spirit, so free and unfettered in its charismatic gifts to the Church through religious life.

Nevertheless, I see that this aspect of Church life is still alive under the Spirit and for that I am grateful and see it as a positive sign of hope.

CONCLUSION

More than anything else, human beings are the bearers of the Spirit and the true signs of hope in our midst. Everyone could make a list of people who have shown that life of the Spirit to them, who have been their personal living signs of hope. Each one of us has different needs and also a different vision. I will betray my own by the list I give of people who have been signs of hope for me. In keeping with an old Church practice, I will list only deceased persons.

Two popes will take their place on my list, Pope John XXIII and Pope Paul VI. They were such different people but complemented each other by their gifts. John XXIII was a historian and because of that knowledge of history had the broader vision of the Church. The calling of Vatican Council II came out of his sense of history. To his vision I am forever grateful. Paul VI was a delicate soul, more melancholy, more philosophical by natural bent. But he had a sensitivity to people and a warm heart, a humility and dignity that has always made him esteemed. He was, in addition, a Benedictine at heart.

Barbara Ward and Oscar Romero have been people of hope for me. My first real introduction to social justice on an international basis came through the speech of Barbara Ward at the synod of bishops in 1971 and through her many writings which I subsequently devoured. She helped form the theoretical basis for my thinking and stimulated a lively interest in the inequalities that mark our globe. Oscar Romero is in a different category. He is to me the model of an honest and sincere person who thus had the inner capabilities of change. I admired his courage, his persistence, his forthrightness. He remains a sign of hope to me.

In addition, I could name many of the Benedictine confreres I have had the privilege to live with or be associated with, both in my own monastery and as head of the Benedictine Order. These people, known to only a few, were pillars of strength to me and remain models of how the discipleship of Christ is to be lived out in any age. They exemplified the Benedictine synthesis of piety, learning, joy, art, and caring that have marked the monastic charism. Underneath all the talk about religious life, I came to realize that it really meant the chance to follow Christ with others of like mind, to be daily strengthened by scripture, to see the whole of life like a school of unselfish service in the Kingdom. There were many heroes in that life.

I have also come to see many models and heroes in my own archdiocese of Milwaukee. They are to me signs of hope. I see them among the clergy and among the laity, among the ecumenical partners and among the various business and civic officials. It is not always easy to live with heroes and models of hope—they can be difficult people—but they have taught me the lesson of how the gospel, in the reality of everyday life, relates to this world. They have taught me in the concrete how faith relates to the daily human enterprise. They are signs that the Spirit is alive in our midst.

Notes

PART I

1. Karl Rahner, "Towards a Fundamental Theological Interpretation of Vatican II," *Theological Studies* 40 (1979) 716–27.

1. NOSTALGIA WITH A FUTURE

1. This chapter is based on a conference given in Albany, New York, on Dec. 16, 1988, on the occasion of the twenty-fifth anniversary of the ordination to the priesthood of Bishop Howard Hubbard.

2. The literature on Vatican Council II and its effects is abundant. The most thorough scholarly article on the position of Vatican II in the history of the Church is: "Developments, Reforms, and Two Great Reformations: Towards a Historical Assessment of Vatican II," by John W. O'Malley, S.J., *Theological Studies* 44 (1983), pp. 373-406. Older, but still useful, tools are: *Dictionary of the Council*, edited by J. Deretz and A. Nocent, O.S.B., Washington D.C.: Corpus Books, 1968; *Commentary on the Documents of Vatican II*, edited by Herbert Vorgrimler, 5 vol., New York: Herder and Herder, 1967-69.

The following books give the spirit of the period before and immediately following the Council and, in addition to those by Xavier Rynne cited later, were eagerly read by so many of us: Hans Küng, *The Council: Reform and Reunion*, New York: Sheed & Ward, 1961; Michael Novak, *The Open Church: Vatican II, Act II*, New York: Macmillan, 1962-64; Mario von Galli, *The Council and the Future*, New York: McGraw Hill, 1966; Bernhard Häring, *Road to Renewal: Perspectives of Vatican II*, New York: Alba House, 1966; Ralph M. Wiltger, S.V.D., *The Rhine Flows into the Tiber: The Unknown Council*, New York: Hawthorn Books, 1967; Thomas F. O'Dea, *The Catholic Crisis*, Boston: Beacon Press, 1968; Bishop Christopher Butler, *In the Light of the Council*, London: Darton, Longman & Todd, 1969; Peter Hebblethwaite, *The Runaway Church: Post-conciliar Growth or Decline*, New York: Seabury Press, 1975; Karol Cardinal Wojtyla, *Sources of Renewal: The Implementation of the Second Vatican Council*, San Francisco: Harper & Row, 1980; Bishop Christopher Butler, *The Theology of Vatican II*, Westminster, Md.: Christian Classics, Inc., 1981 (a rewriting of his earlier book of 1969). More recent books show the change of tone as the Council is assessed twenty or more years later: Joseph Gremillion, ed., *The Church and Culture Since Vatican II: The Experience of North and Latin America*, Notre Dame, Ind.: University of Notre Dame Press, 1985; Alberic Stacpoole, ed., *Vatican II Revisited by Those Who Were There*, Minneapolis, Minn.: Winston Press, 1986; Lucien Richard, O.S.I., Daniel T. Harrington, S.J., and John W. O'Malley, S.J. eds., *Vatican II: The Unfinished Agenda*, New York: Paulist Press, 1987; *The*

162

Reception of Vatican II, ed. by Giuseppe Alberigo, Jean-Pierre Jossua, and Joseph Komonchak, trans. by Matthew J. O'Connell, Washington, D.C.: Catholic University of America Press, 1987; *The Church in Anguish: Has the Vatican Betrayed Vatican II?*, edited by Hans Küng and Leonard Swidler, San Francisco: Harper & Row, 1988; Avery R. Dulles, *The Reshaping of Catholicism: Current Challenges in the Theology of the Church*, San Francisco: Harper & Row, 1988; John W. O'Malley, *Tradition and Transition: Historical Perspectives on Vatican II*, Wilmington, Del.: M. Glazier, 1989.

3. There are several editions of the documents of Vatican Council II in English: *The Documents of Vatican II (1962-1965)*, edited by Walter M. Abbott, New York: Herder & Herder, 1966; Austin Flannery, ed., *Vatican Council II: The Conciliar and Post Conciliar Documents*, Grand Rapids, Mich.: Wm. B. Eerdmans Publishing Co., 1982; Norman P. Tanner, S.J., ed., *Decrees of the Ecumenical Councils*, 2 vols., Washington, D.C.: Georgetown University Press, 1990.

4. Four volumes of *Letters from Vatican City* by Xavier Rynne (pseud.) appeared between 1963 and 1966. These were gathered into one volume entitled *Vatican Council II*, New York: Straus & Giroux, 1968.

5. Tanner, *Decrees of the Ecumenical Councils*, vol. 2, p. 20.

6. Avery R. Dulles, S.J., uses ten categories to sum up the special emphasis of Vatican II in *The Reshaping of Catholicism*, San Francisco: Harper & Row, 1988, pp. 19-33: 1. Aggiornamento; 2. Reformability of the Church; 3. Renewed Attention to the Word of God; 4. Collegiality; 5. Religious Freedom; 6. The Active Role of the Laity; 7. Regional and Local Variety; 8. Ecumenism; 9. Dialogue with other Religions; and 10. The Social Mission of the Church. Since Father Dulles writes, "Who does not accept all ten of these principles, I contend, cannot honestly claim to have accepted the results of Vatican II," I hasten to make my affirmation of faith in all ten, but I have reduced them for convenience sake to the four that seem the most central to me.

7. *The Ratzinger Report: An Exclusive Interview on the State of the Church by Joseph Cardinal Ratzinger with Vittorio Messori*, Salvator Attanasio and Graham Harrison, trans., San Francisco: Ignatius Press, 1985. On p. 38 the Cardinal states that he understands "restoration" as a "recovery of lost values," or "a newly found balance of orientations and values within the Catholic totality." He strongly denies that it means a rejection of Vatican II or a rewriting of history.

8. Pope John Paul II, "The Call of the Extraordinary Synod," in *The Extraordinary Synod—1985*, Boston: St. Paul Editions, 1985, pp. 18-19.

9. See Dulles, *Reshaping*, "The Extraordinary Synod of 1985," pp. 184-206.

2. CATHOLICISM TODAY

1. This essay was first published in the *National Catholic Reporter*, Oct, 13, 1989, pp. 1, 14–16, and reprinted in French in *La Documentation catholique*, n. 1997, Jan. 1990, pp. 34–39.

2. Karl Rahner, "Towards a Fundamental Theological Interpretation of Vatican II," *Theological Studies* 40 (1979): 716-27.

3. These entities have now become a part of Church Law and are found in the revised Code of Canon Law of 1983: on the Synods of Bishops, canon 334, and canons 342-348; on the Conferences of Bishops, canons 447-459.

4. Having been in Rome during the Synod of 1967 and having myself been a

member of the Synods of 1969, 1971, and 1974, I can attest that they still were held under the glow and the impetus of the council itself. The first two were less focused and dealt with a variety of points implementing documents of Vatican II. That of 1971 had two themes: the ministerial priesthood and justice in the modern world. The Synod of 1974 became even more specific, focusing on evangelization. Since then each synod has had a more restrictive theme. Having been a member of the Synod of 1987, I can also attest that the spirit of Vatican Council II is dead in the synods, and they have become heavy and ineffectual, if not counterproductive.

5. For a survey of the many questions now being posed about the nature and authority of the national Conferences of Bishops, see Thomas J. Reese, S.J., *Episcopal Conferences: Historical, Canonical, and Theological Studies*, Washington, D.C.: Georgetown University Press, 1989.

6. Canon 454 states: "#1. Diocesan bishops, those equivalent to them in law and also coadjutor bishops, have a deliberative vote in plenary sessions of the conference of bishops by the law itself. #2. Auxiliary bishops and other titular bishops who are members of the episcopal conference enjoy either a deliberative or consultative vote according to the prescriptions of the statutes of the conference; however, only those mentioned in #1 enjoy a deliberative vote when it is a question of drawing up or modifying the statues."

7. Much discussion in this vein took place here in the Archdiocese of Milwaukee between the publication of the first draft of a pastoral letter, *Facing the Future with Hope*, in January 1991 and the final draft in November of that same year.

3. THE KINGDOM OF GOD AND THIS WORLD

1. This chapter is a conflation of several talks given in 1991, the one hundredth anniversary of *Rerum novarum*. That year saw a renewed interest in Catholic social teaching.

2. Most of the encyclicals of John Paul II, even when they are not explicitly on social doctrine, have passages that are pertinent to that theme. This was true of the very first encyclical, *Redemptor hominis* (1979), and of many others. The three that are explicitly social in character are: *Laborem exercens* (1981), *Sollicitudo rei socialis* (1988), and *Centesimus annus* (1991).

3. See, in particular, the splendid study by Paul Misner, *Social Catholicism in Europe*, New York: Crossroad Publishing Co., 1991.

4. The famous quote is: "As history abundantly proves, it is true that on account of changed conditions many things which were done by small associations in former times cannot be done now save by large associations. Still, that most weighty principle, which cannot be set aside or changed, remains fixed and unshaken in social philosophy: Just as it is gravely wrong to take from individuals what they can accomplish by their own initiative and industry and give it to the community, so also it is an injustice and at the same time a grave evil and disturbance of right order to assign to a greater and higher association what lesser and subordinate organizations can do. For every social activity ought of its very nature to furnish help to the members of the body social, and never destroy and absorb them" (*Quadragesimo anno*, #79).

5. Pope Pius XII pointed out the validity of subsidiarity "even for the life of the Church, without prejudice to its hierarchical structure" (Address to the College of Cardinals, Feb. 20, 1946, *Acta Apostolicae Sedis* 38 [1946]: 141–51).

6. Peter J. Henriot, Edward P. DeBerri, and Michael J. Schultheis, *Catholic Social Teaching: Our Best Kept Secret,* third revised edition, Maryknoll, N.Y.: Orbis Books, 1992, pp. 22–25.

7. George E. McCarthy and Royal W. Rhodes, *Eclipse of Justice: Ethics, Economics, and the Lost Traditions of American Catholicism,* Maryknoll, N.Y.: Orbis Books, 1992, pp. 152–54.

8. Walter Kasper, *Jesus the Christ,* New York, N.Y.: Paulist Press, 1977, p. 265.

9. Ibid., p. 265.

10. *Centesimus annus,* #25.

11. *Justice in the World,* #6.

12. *Centesimus annus,* #5.

13. *Economic Justice for All,* #135.

14. *Centesimus annus,* #3.

4. RELIGION AND PUBLIC POLICY

1. This article is the substance of a conference delivered at St. Vincent College, Latrobe, Pennsylvania, December 6, 1983.

2. *New York Times,* Nov. 28, 1983, 16.

3. *De ordine,* Book 2, chapter 4. *The Fathers of the Church,* vol. 5, 1948, pp. 287–88.

4. *Summa theologica,* I^a, I^{ae}, q. 96, a. 2.

5. "Religion and Power in America Today," *Commonweal,* 2 Dec. 1982, 650–51.

6. See in particular section 36 of that document.

7. "Tolerance and Truth in America," reprinted in *Origins,* vol. 13, no. 23, 396–99. An unsigned and undated memorandum from the Congregation for the Doctrine of the Faith was sent to all the bishops of the U.S.A. in June of 1992. It bore the cumbersome title: "Some Considerations Concerning the Catholic Response to Legislative Proposals on the Non-discrimination of Homosexual Persons." One would have to say that it falls into the integralist position described in this chapter.

8. See in particular Maritain, *Integral Humanism: Temporal and Spiritual Problems of a New Christendom,* Joseph W. Evans, trans. (Notre Dame University Press, Notre Dame, Ind., 1973). This work appeared in French in 1936 under the title: *Humanisme intégral.* In addition to John Courtney Murray's *We Hold These Truths: Catholic Reflections on the American Proposition,* New York: Sheed and Ward, 1960, I find the following two articles by the same author of special importance, since they span the debate of Vatican Council II on Religious Liberty: "The Problem of Religious Freedom," *Theological Studies,* 25 (1964), 503-74, and "The Issue of Church and State at Vatican Council II," *Theological Studies,* 27 (1966), 580-606.

9. It would have been helpful if the bishops at the Council had explained how they understood the phrase "within due limits." It is not clear how force can be used against any conscience. In so many ways it was unfortunate that this phrase, which defies understanding, was added to the document.

I have found most useful for this section the unpublished conference by Father Bryan Hehir to the Workshop on Church-State Relations at the General Meeting of the NCCB-USCC, November 13, 1978, "Catholic Theology of Church and State: An Analysis of Basic Concepts." Moreover, I have found helpful the chapter on John Courtney Murray, S.J., in Father Charles Curran's work: *American Catholic*

Social Ethics: Twentieth-Century Approaches, (Notre Dame, Ind.: University of Notre Dame Press, 1982), pp. 172–232.

5. THE CHURCH IN WORLDLY AFFAIRS

1. This article first appeared in *America*, Oct. 18, 1986: 201–5, 215–16.

2. *The Challenge of Peace: God's Promise and Our Response*, Pastoral Letter of the United States Bishops, 1983, and *Economic Justice for All: Catholic Social Teaching and the U.S. Economy*, Pastoral Letter of the United States Bishops, 1986.

6. PRINCIPLES FOR THE RELATION OF CHURCH AND GOVERNMENT

1. This chapter was an address to the Wisconsin State Assembly, Feb. 5, 1987.

2. "Pastoral Message," #27.

3. *The Church in the Modern World*, #40.

4. *Declaration on Religious Liberty*, #1.

5. "Pastoral Message," #18.

PART III

1. After *Humanae vitae*, Pope Paul VI did not write any more encyclicals. This document is entitled an Apostolic Letter to give it a lesser degree of authority. This was not done because Pope Paul was less secure about its contents but rather because he did not want to use his highest teaching authority again, namely, the category of encyclical. Immediately after his installation, Pope John Paul II returned to the encyclical as his primary teaching tool.

2. *Octogesima adveniens*, #4.

3. The literature discussing the Economic Pastoral Letter is most extensive. The best bibliography is found in the excellent and provocative study by George E. McCarthy and Royal W. Rhodes, *Eclipse of Justice: Ethics, Economics, and the Lost Traditions of American Catholicism*, Maryknoll, N.Y.: Orbis Books, 1992, n. 2, p. 244. Among the more substantial negative criticisms, I would like to single out that by Douglas Rasmussen, "The Morality of Power and the Power of Morality," in Charles R. Strain, ed., *Prophetic Visions and Economic Realities: Protestants, Jews, and Catholics Confront the Bishops' Letter on the Economy*, Grand Rapids, Mich.: Wm. B. Eerdmans Publishing Co., 1989, pp. 134-45.

4. For a discussion of the differences between the bishops' approach and that of Professor Rawls, see: McCarthy and Rhodes, *Eclipse*, pp. 87–93, 99–103.

7. GOD AND MAMMON

1. The text of this article is from a conference delivered at the National Catholic Education Association Convention, St. Louis, Missouri, April 11, 1985.

2. *Mater et Magistra*, #40.

3. Address to the Bishops of Brazil, *Origins* 10:9 (July 31, 1980): 135.

8. TOWARD A MORAL EVALUATION OF THE ECONOMY

1. Although this article may seem outdated, the factors related in it are just as relevant in our day. The question of poverty has not gone away; in fact, it has grown

worse. These remarks are also a brief summary of some of the more important points raised by the bishops in their letter and thus worth reflecting on again and again.

9. HOW TO READ THE ECONOMIC PASTORAL

1. This article appeared in *Crisis*, 4 (1986): 27–34. Since it was written between the second and third drafts of the Economic Pastoral Letter, it has some historical interest. It shows much of the inner workings of the drafting committee as it reacted to the feedback that kept coming its way. So many of the descriptions of the economic situation then have not changed much in the ensuing years. It also shows that each draft of the letter had a life of its own and that many good features had to be abandoned because of the need to shorten the letter and to make it more acceptable to the body of bishops.

2. Joseph Cardinal Ratzinger with Vittorio Messori, trans. by Salvator Attanasio and Graham Harrison, *The Ratzinger Report: An Exclusive Interview of the State of the Church*, San Francisco: Ignatius Press, 1985. See, in particular, pp. 155–69.

3. *Gaudium et spes*, #42.

4. *Gaudium et spes*, #72.

5. *Gaudium et spes*, #40.

6. *Catholic Social Teaching and the U.S. Economy*, draft 2, #32, *Origins*, 15 (1985): 261.

7. *Justice in the Marketplace*, U.S. Catholic Conference, 1985, p. 42.

8. *Catholic Social Teaching and the U.S. Economy*, draft 2, #46.

9. Ibid., #285.

10. ECONOMIC JUSTICE AND THE AMERICAN TRADITION

1. This chapter appeared first in Italian as the preface to the Italian edition of the U.S. Catholic Bishops' Economic Pastoral Letter: *Giustizia economica per tutti*, Rome: Edizioni Lavoro, 1987. It was republished in the periodical of the International Institute Jacques Maritain, *Notes et Documents*, 19/20 (1987): 87–106. The version presented here has been shortened slightly to avoid repetitions.

2. *The Tablet*, March 8, 1986: 246.

3. Herbert McClosky and John Zaller, *The American Ethos: Attitudes Toward Capitalism and Democracy*, Cambridge, Mass.: Harvard University Press, 1984, p. 1.

4. Ibid., p. 7.

5. Berkeley, 1985, p. 256.

6. Ibid., p. 250.

11. THE ECONOMIC PASTORAL LETTER REVISITED

1. This article first appeared in: John A. Coleman, S.J., ed., *One Hundred Years of Catholic Social Thought: Celebration and Challenge*, Maryknoll, N.Y.: Orbis Books, 1991, pp. 201–11.

2. *L'Osservatore Romano* (German edition) 29 Nov. 1985; *L'Osservatore Romano* (English edition) 23 Dec. 1985.

3. *Revista Eclesiastica Brasileira*, 47 (June 1987): 356–77.

4. A fine and balanced analysis of this question can be found in Arthur F.

McGovern, S.J., "Latin America and Dependency Theory," *This World*, (Spring–Summer 1986): 104–23.

12. SIGNS OF THE SPIRIT IN OUR AGE

1. These remarks were the basis of a talk to the priests of the Archdiocese of Milwaukee, May 19, 1992.

2. *Lumen gentium*, #12.

3. John H. Newman, *On Consulting the Faithful in Matters of Doctrine*, Kansas City, MO: Sheed and Ward, 1961.

4. *Lumen gentium*, #22.

5. *Lumen gentium*, #27.

6. *Presbyterorum ministerio*, #2.

7. *Presbyterorum ministerio*, #2.

8. *Presbyterorum ministerio*, #7.

9. *Centesimus annus*, #5.

10. *Pacem in terris*, #41.

11. *Inter insigniores*, par. 5, *Origins*, vol. 6, p. 522.